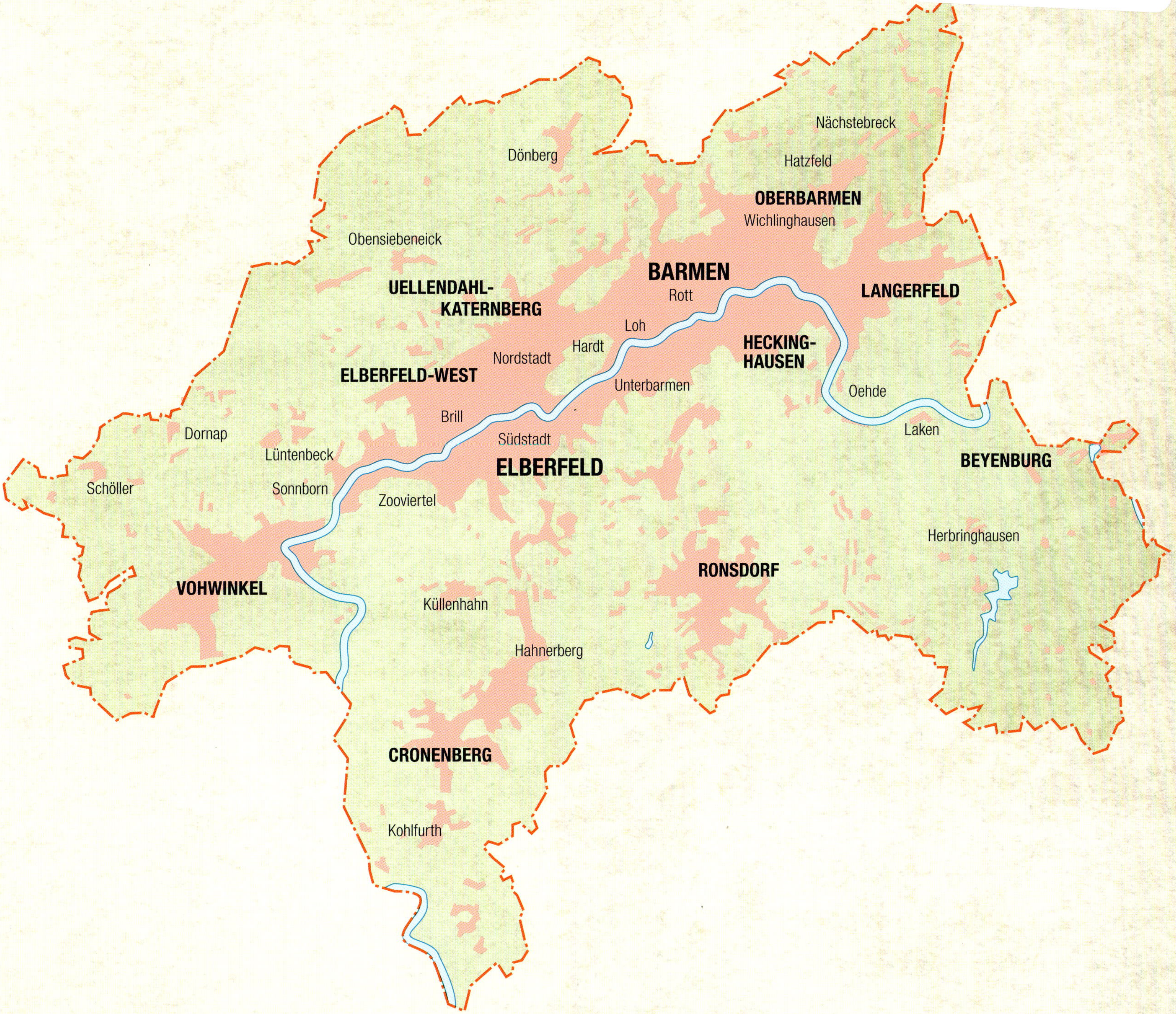
Nächstebreck
Dönberg
Hatzfeld
OBERBARMEN
Wichlinghausen
Obensiebeneick
BARMEN
UELLENDAHL-
KATERNBERG
Rott
LANGERFELD
Loh
HECKING-
HAUSEN
Hardt
Nordstadt
ELBERFELD-WEST
Unterbarmen
Oehde
Brill
Südstadt
Laken
Dornap
Lüntenbeck
ELBERFELD
BEYENBURG
Schöller
Sonnborn
Zooviertel
Herbringhausen
RONSDORF
VOHWINKEL
Küllenhahn
Hahnerberg
CRONENBERG
Kohlfurth

Übersicht

Karte der Bezirke	1, 172
Einleitung	4 - 5
Bilder mit Beschreibungen	8 - 169

Motive nach Stadtteil	Seiten
Oberbarmen	8 - 9, 14 - 19
Heckinghausen	8 - 13
Barmen	20 - 66, 70, 74, 158 - 159
Elberfeld	67 - 65, 67 - 131
Vohwinkel	132- 141
Cronenberg	142 - 148
Ronsdorf	149 - 157
Langerfeld	160 - 165
Beyenburg	159, 166 - 169

Impressum	170
Literaturverzeichnis	171

Index

Citymap with Districts	*1, 172*
Introduction	*6 - 7*
Images with descriptions	*8 - 169*

Images by Districts	*Pages*
Oberbarmen	*8 - 9, 14 - 19*
Heckinghausen	*8 - 13*
Barmen	*20 - 66, 70, 74, 158 - 159*
Elberfeld	*67 - 65, 67 - 131*
Vohwinkel	*132- 141*
Cronenberg	*142 - 148*
Ronsdorf	*149 - 157*
Langerfeld	*160 - 165*
Beyenburg	*159, 166 - 169*

Imprint	*170*
Bibliography	*171*

Dieses Buch ist der Erinnerung an Hans Joachim de Bruyn-Ouboter (1947 – 2016) gewidmet.

Der Wuppertaler Oberstudienrat a.D. fühlte sich als Historiker der Geschichte der Bergischen Region besonders verbunden.
Er war Leiter des Referats für Denkmal- und Stadtbildpflege des Bergischen Geschichtsvereins (BGV), Vorsitzender der BGV-Abteilung Wuppertal und Mitglied im Beirat des Rheinischen Vereins für Denkmalpflege und Landschaftsschutz.
Seine Forschungsergebnisse liegen in zahlreichen Veröffentlichungen zur Geschichte und Architektur in Wuppertal vor.
Verlag und Autorin danken Frau Ingeborg de Bruyn-Ouboter herzlich, auf das publizierte Wissen ihres Mannes zurückgreifen zu können.

Wuppertal Portrait einer Stadt

Fotos: Holger Klaes

Texte: Gisela Schmoeckel

klaes-regio

„Mais c'est un ange" - „Aber das ist ja ein Engel!"

Jean Cocteau 1889-1963 beim Anblick der Schwebebahn während seines Besuches in Wuppertal Anfang der 1950er Jahre

Wuppertal - viel mehr als eine Schwebebahnstadt

Die Stadt Wuppertal ist eine junge Großstadt. Ende der 1920er Jahre hatten Pläne, das rheinisch-westfälische Industriegebiet neu zu gliedern, zu heftigen Auseinandersetzungen geführt. Aber am 1. August 1929 entstanden durch Zusammenschluss mehrerer Kommunen neue kreisfreie Städte, so auch Wuppertal aus den bis dahin selbständigen Städten Elberfeld und Barmen.

„Elberfeld und Barmen - sind sie nicht wie jene siamesischen Zwillinge, welche, obwohl keineswegs in allen Stücken harmonierend, so fest mit einander verwachsen waren, dass man sie lebendig nicht trennen konnte? Man kann über Barmen nicht schreiben, ohne auch Elberfeld, und über Elberfeld nicht, ohne auch Barmen zu berühren."

Wilhelm Langewiesche schrieb diese Sätze schon 1863 in dem ersten, umfassenden Reiseführer über die Doppelstadt, in dem er Schwerpunkte auf die Darstellung der Industrie und die bergische Geschichte legte. Dem „siamesischen Zwilling" gesellten sich 1929 die auch bis dahin eigenständigen Ortschaften hinzu, wie Vohwinkel, Ronsdorf, Cronenberg und Beyenburg. Der östliche Stadtteil Langerfeld war schon 1922 nach Barmen eingemeindet worden. 1970 vergrößerte sich das Stadtgebiet noch einmal um die Orte Dönberg, Dornap, Obensiebeneick und Schöller im Nordwesten.

Das mächtige und schnelle Anwachsen der Industriestadt seit dem 18. Jahrhundert im Tal der Wupper war der Grund für das große Interesse. Für Friedrich Engels, selbst Sohn eines patriarchalischen Unternehmers in Barmen, war das „Mucker-Tal" das „deutsche Manchester" und die soziale Not der massenhaft zuwandernden Arbeiterfamilien in den Industriestädten der Grund für seine Zusammenarbeit mit Karl Marx und die Entwicklung des wissenschaftlichen Sozialismus.

Dabei hatte noch 1778 der „empfindsame" Dichter, Arzt und Wirtschaftsgelehrte Johann Heinrich Jung-Stilling (1740-1817), ein Freund aus Goethes Studienzeit in Straßburg, über den Blick auf Elberfeld in seiner Jugendzeit geschrieben: „Als er auf die Höhe kam, und die unvergleichliche Stadt mit dem paradiesischen Tal überschaute, so freute er sich, setzte sich hin auf den Rasen, und beschaute das alles eine Weile; hierbei stieg ihm der Wunsch so tief aus dem Innersten seiner Seele empor : Ach Gott! möcht' ich doch da mein Leben beschließen!" Wer heute von der Aussichtsterrasse des Mensagebäudes der Bergischen Universität auf Elberfeld herabschaut, kann sich dieses Paradies kaum noch vorstellen. Aber auf historischen Ansichten, vor allem aus der Romantik, ist das Grün der Talaue mit ihren vielen weißen, zum Bleichen aufgestellten Garngestellen dargestellt.

Aber selbst das vom Qualm der vielen Schornsteine aus den Fabriken mit ihren unzählig vielen Dampfmaschinen verdüsterte Elberfeld wurde weltberühmter touristischer Anziehungspunkt, als die Schwebebahn von 1898 bis 1903 mit ihrem filigranen Stahlgerüst über die Wupper gebaut wurde. Dieses 13,3 Kilometer lange „eiserne Rückgrat" folgt allen Windungen des Flusses und befördert seitdem als „schwebender Paternoster" mit wenigen Ausnahmen und sehr seltenen Unfällen etwa 30 Millionen Fahrgäste im Jahr durch die Stadt. Sie fährt in Vohwinkel über die Straße und hat 20 Haltestellen. Als 1910 die Dichterin Else Lasker-Schüler (1869-1945) ihre Geburtsstadt Elberfeld zur 300Jahrfeier besuchte, schrieb sie: „Ich bin verliebt in meine Stadt und bin stolz auf ihre Schwebebahn, ein Eisengewinde, ein stahlharter Drachen, wendet und legt er sich mit vielen Bahnhofköpfen und sprühenden Augen über den schwarzgefärbten Fluss. Immer fliegt mit Tausendgetöse das Bahnschiff durch die Lüfte über das Wasser auf schweren Ringfüßen. Durch Elberfeld, weiter über Barmen zurück nach Sonnborn-Rittershausen am Zoologischen Garten vorbei" (aus Lasker-Schüler, „Gesichte" 1913). Bis heute ist das Projekt „Schwebebahn" ein pionierhaftes technisches Wunderwerk, das die Bürger der Schwesterstädte, trotz ihrer Konkurrenzsituation, lange vor dem offiziellen Zusammenschluss gemeinsam errichteten.

Aus der Geschichte

Seit den spektakulären frühgeschichtlichen Funden bei der Anlage einer Tiefgarage unter dem Elberfelder Park „deWeerth'scher Garten" im Jahr 2003, ist eine Besiedlung im Tal der Wupper schon in der Eisenzeit, im 6. bis 4. Jahrhundert vor Christus gesichert. Nachgewiesen ist kontinuierliche Besiedlung seit dem 8. Jahrhundert, mit dem Beginn der Sachsenkriege Karls des Großen. Grabungsfunde zeigen, dass um 950 schon in Elberfeld eine Kirche gestanden hat, um 1040 wird Cronenberg zum ersten Mal urkundlich erwähnt. Seit dem 11. Jahrhundert gehörten weite Teile der späteren Stadt zur Grafschaft, dem späteren Herzogtum Berg. Im 15. Jahrhundert lieferten Elberfelder und Barmer Bleicher Leinengarn an Kölner Kaufleute. Aus diesem frühen Textilgewerbe entstand die erfolgreiche, auf viele verschiedene Produkte spezialisierte Textilindustrie, von der Schmalbandweberei vor allem in Barmen, Langerfeld und Ronsdorf, bis zur Massenkonfektion in Elberfeld. Ende des 19. Jahrhunderts war die Elberfelder „Hofaue" eines der größten Textilhandelszentren der Welt. Aus den Garnbleichereien und Garnfärbereien entwickelten sich Maschinenbau und die Chemische Industrie. Der weltweit agierende Bayer-Konzern entstand in Heckinghausen und Elberfeld, wo heute noch die Schwebebahn durch die Produktionsanlagen beim Zoo fährt.

Das Stadtbild

Als einmalige „Kombination von Bandstadt und Mittelgebirgsstadt" bezeichnete Hans Joachim de Bruyn-Ouboter die Stadt, die sich am Ufer des Flusses und den oft sehr steilen Berghängen bildete. Sie wuchs zusammen aus den verschiedensten Ortschaften, die jeweils bis heute ihre eigene Struktur und auch Aussehen behalten haben. Die Wohlhabenheit der Bürger ließ im 17. Jahrhundert den typischen „bergischen" Baustil mit seinen barocken Elementen in dem Dreifarbenakkord Grün, weiß und Schiefergrau entstehen. Um die Jahrhundertwende errichteten Fabrikanten und Banker das im

Zweiten Weltkrieg nicht zerstörte Villenviertel „Brill", das viele Touristen anzieht. Auch wenn heute Elberfeld Hauptzentrum der Stadt bildet, hat Barmen eine lebendige, liebenswerte City erhalten. Verheerende Bombenangriffe auf Barmen und Elberfeld im Jahr 1943 zerstörten weitgehend die Innenstädte, insgesamt fast 40 % der gesamten Bausubstanz. Beim Wiederaufbau fielen viele erhaltene Gebäude und Straßen zusätzlich dem Ziel einer „autogerechten" Stadt zum Opfer. Erst seit den 1970er Jahren konnte ein Umdenken zu Gunsten des Denkmalschutzes das atmosphäre Bild alter Stadtviertel retten. Bis auf Beyenburg, das seinen dörflichen Charakter durch die Klosteranlage behalten hat, sind die übrigen Wuppertaler Stadtteile in der Geschichte stark durch die verschiedenen Ausformungen des protestantischen, evangelischen Glaubens geprägt. Früher galt sie als sektenreichste Stadt Deutschlands, durch die Zuwanderung vieler Menschen aus katholischen Regionen hat sich das evangelische Übergewicht ausgeglichen. Heute ist Wuppertal eine Stadt von Menschen vieler verschiedener Herkunftsländer und Kulturen.

Zahlen

1708-9 hatten Elberfeld und Barmen zusammen ca. 5 800 Einwohner, 1863 waren es 106 065, um 1900 war die Zahl auf 360 000 angewachsen. Mit 430 000 Einwohnern im Jahr 1963 fühlte man sich auf dem Weg zur Halbmillionen-Stadt. Aber durch Sterben der deutschen Textilindustrie und der allgemeinen demographischen Entwicklung ging die Bevölkerung zurück. Nach letzter Zählung hatte Wuppertal 2016 rund 351 000 Einwohner. Der höchste Berg im Stadtgebiet ist der Lichtscheid im Süden Barmens mit einer Höhe von 350 Metern, tiefster Punkt wird an der Wupper in Müngsten mit 100 Metern gemessen. Die Länge der Wupper im Stadtgebiet beträgt 33,9 Kilometer, die enge Bebauung des Tals führte zu einer extrem hohen Zahl von über 100 Brücken. Fast 500 Treppen bilden schnelle Verbindungswege zwischen den Straßen an den steilen Berghängen für Fußgänger. Treppen und Brücken, das Schwebebahngerüst und viele Grünanlagen, die immer stadtnah erreichbar sind, prägen das Stadtbild. „Großstadt im Grünen" war früher ein Werbeslogan.

Universitätsstadt

Die spezialisierte, vielfältige Industrieproduktion brauchte gute Ausbildungsmöglichkeiten. Erste Lateinschule, aus der später im 19. Jahrhundert die Gymnasien, Real- und Höheren Bürgerschulen entstanden, wurde in Elberfeld 1592 gegründet, in Barmen entstand 1596 eine erste Amtsschule als Mittelpunktschule für die verstreuten Höfe. Seit 1863 bildete die Höhere Gewerbeschule Ingenieure aus, die 1898 zur Königlich Vereinigten Maschinenbauschule Elberfeld-Barmen wurde. 1894 und 1897 entstanden die Barmer und die Elberfelder Kunstgewerbeschulen, 1897 die Königlich-Preußische Baugewerkschule für Elberfeld-Barmen und 1900 folgte die Preußische Höhere Fachschule für die Textilindustrie in Barmen. Die Pädagogische Akademie Wuppertal wurde 1946 gegründet und gehörte seit 1965 zu den Pädagogischen Hochschulen Rheinland. Die Werkkunstschule seit 1946, das Institut für Industrieformen, Industrial Design und die Höhere Fachschule für die Grafische Industrie wurden Schwerpunkte in der Wuppertaler Berufsausbildung. Der Initiative des damaligen NRW-Ministerpräsidenten, späteren Bundespräsidenten Johannes Rau (1931-2006) ist es zu verdanken, dass 1972 in Wuppertal eine Gesamthochschule gegründet wurde, in die sich diese Fachausbildungsinstiute integrierten. Seit 2003 ist die „Bergische Universität mit ihrem Campus am Grifflenberg stadtbildprägend.

Weltberühmt wurde Wuppertal nicht nur durch seine Industrieprodukte, sondern als Missionsstadt. In Südafrika hat eine 1832 als Missionsstation gegründete Kleinstadt am Westkap den Namen „Wupperthal". 1828 wurde auf der Hardt, dem Bergrücken, auf dem sich heute der Botanische Garten befindet, die Rheinische Missionsgesellschaft gegründet. Hier wurden Missionare ausgebildet und ausgesendet, um in den Kolonien für den Evangelischen Glauben zu missionieren. Von dort brachten Missionare Kultobjekte der einheimischen Ethnien mit und es entstand eine bemerkenswerte, reiche völkerkundliche Sammlung. Diese ist im „Museum auf der Hardt" zu besichtigen.

Sinn für Kulturpflege, Freude am Opern-, Theater und Konzertleben entfaltete sich im Lauf des 19. Jahrhunderts. Die großartige, repräsentative Historische Stadthalle in Elberfeld ist ein Zeugnis dieses Bürgersinns. Ende des 19. Jahrhunderts gründeten in Barmen und in Elberfeld kunstliebende Bürgervereine Kunstsammlungen. 1908 kaufte der Elberfelder Bankier August von der Heydt von Picasso das erste Bild, das der damals junge vielversprechende Maler an ein Museum verkaufen konnte. „Akrobat und junger Halekin" war bis 1937 im Elberfelder, dem heutigen Von der Heydt-Museum zu sehen. Es wurde zusammen mit mehr als 500 Bildern durch die Nationalsozialisten beschlagnahmt und konnte nie mehr nach Wuppertal zurückkehren. Doch nach dem Krieg wurde das Wuppertaler von der Heydt-Museum eines der profiliertesten Museen Westdeutschlands und konnte sehr sehenswerte Sammlungen wieder aufbauen. Künstler der Avantgarde fanden in der Stadt eine Heimat. So erarbeitete Pina Bausch (1940-2009) mit ihrem Ensemble die weltberühmten, revolutionären Choreographien des Tanztheaters Wuppertal und der aus England stammende Bildhauer Tony Cragg hat hier sein Atelier und seine Werkstätten. Seit 2008 zieht sein „Skulpturenpark Waldfrieden" aus aller Welt viele Freunde der zeitgenössischen Kunst an. Das Museum für Frühindustrialisierung und Engelshaus in Barmen, die Bergischen Museumsbahnen in der Kohlfurth an der Wupper zeigen Technik- und Industriegeschichte. Heute ist Wuppertal eine wie früher von mittelständischer Industrie geprägter Ort mit vielen Berufsbildern aus dem Design- und Kreativbereichen. Eine Attraktion aus jüngster Zeit ist die Nordbahntrasse. Sie führt seit 2014 über Viadukte, durch Tunnel und Schluchten auf dem Gleisbett der früher im Norden an der Stadt vorbeiführenden Eisenbahn, der 23 Kilometer langen Rheinischen Strecke und ist ein attraktiver, schneller Rad- und Fußweg geworden. Zu danken ist diese Trasse mit vielen großartigen Ausblicken auf die Stadt der „Wupper-Bewegung" e.V., einer vehement kämpfenden Bürgerinitiative.

„Mais c'est un ange!" - "But that is an angel!"

Jean Cocteau (1889-1963) during his visit to Wuppertal at the beginning of the 1950s

Wuppertal – much more than a suspension railway city

The city of Wuppertal is a young city. At the end of the 1920s plans to restructure the Rhenish-Westphalian industrial area led to fierce clashes. But new independent cities evolved on August 1, 1929 created by the merger of several municipalities just as Wuppertal did from the formerly independent cities of Elberfeld and Barmen.

"Elberfeld and Barmen - are they not like those Siamese twins who, though by no means harmonizing in every way, were so firmly united with one another that they could not be separated alive? One cannot write about Barmen without Elberfeld, as well, and about Elberfeld without not touching on Barmen. "

Wilhelm Langewiesche wrote these sentences as early as 1863 in the first, comprehensive guide to the double city in which he focused on the representation of industry and Bergisch history. The "Siamese twins" were joined in 1929 by villages such as Vohwinkel, Ronsdorf, Cronenberg and Beyenburg that had been independent until then. The eastern district Langerfeld had been incorporated into Barmen in 1922. The city was increased again in 1970 by the villages Dönberg, Dornap, Obensiebeneick and Schöller in the northwest.

The powerful and rapid growth of the industrial city since the 18th century in the 13 km long valley of the Wupper was the reason for the great interest. The "Mucker Valley" (a pietistic sect) was the "German Manchester" for Friedrich Engels, son of a patriarchal entrepreneur in Barmen, and the social distress of the mass immigrant working-class families in the industrial cities the reason for his cooperation with Karl Marx and the development of scientific socialism.

The "sensitive" poet, doctor and economist Johann Heinrich Jung-Stilling (1740-1817), a friend from Goethe's time as a student in Strasbourg had written about the view of Elberfeld in 1778: "When he came to the heights, and he looked over the incomparable city with its paradisiacal valley, he was so happy, sat down on the lawn, and watched it all for a while; desire rose so deep from the innermost of his soul thereby: Oh God! I would like to end my life there! "Anyone looking down from the observation deck of the cafeteria building of the Bergisch University in Elberfeld can hardly imagine this paradise. But in historical views, especially from Romanticism, the green of the floodplain is portrayed with its many white yarn frames set up for bleaching.

But even Elberfeld clouded by the smoke of the many chimneys from the factories with their countless number of steam engines became a world famous tourist attraction as the suspension railway was built from 1898 to 1903 with its filigree steel scaffolding over the Wupper. This 13.3 kilometre "iron backbone" follows all the meanders of the river and has transported about 30 million passengers a year through the city as a "floating paternoster" with rarely an accident. It crosses the street in Vohwinkel and has 20 stops. When the poet Else Lasker-Schüler (1869-1945) visited her hometown Elberfeld in 1910 for the 300th anniversary, she wrote: "I am in love with my city and I am proud of its suspension railway, an iron thread, a steely dragon that turns and places itself with many station heads and sparkling eyes over the black coloured river. The train ship always flies through the skies over the water on heavy ring feet with thousands of roars. Through Elberfeld, continue over Barmen back to Sonnborn-Rittershausen past the zoological garden." (Lasker-Schüler, "Gesichte ",1913)

The project "Suspension Railway" is still a pioneering technical marvel today that the citizens of the sister cities built together long before the official merger and despite their competitive situation.

History

A settlement in the valley of the Wupper as early as the Iron Age in the 6th to 4th centuries BC has been verified ever since the spectacular prehistoric finds during the construction of an underground car park under the Elberfeld park "deWeerth'scher Garten" in 2003. A continuous settlement since the 8th century, with the start of the Saxon wars of Charlemagne, has been proven. Archaeological finds show that there was already a church in Elberfeld in 950, Cronenberg is mentioned in a document for the first time around 1040. Large parts of the later city had belonged to the county, the later Duchy of Berg, since the 11th century. In the 15th century Elberfeld and Barmen delivered bleacher linen yarn to merchants in Cologne. The successful textile industry specializing in many different products, from narrow-band weaving, especially in Barmen, Langerfeld and Ronsdorf, to mass-produced clothing in Elberfeld emerged from this early textile sector. The Elberfeld Hofaue was one of the largest textile trading centres in the world at the end of the 19th century. Mechanical engineering and the chemical industry developed from the yarn bleaching and yarn dyeing. The globally operating Bayer Group was founded in Heckinghausen and Elberfeld, where today the monorail continues through the production facilities at the zoo.

Cityscape

Hans Joachim de Bruyn-Ouboter described the city as a unique "combination of band town and low mountain town" which formed on the bank of the river and the often very steep mountain slopes. It grew together from a variety of localities, each of which has retained its own structure and appearance until today.

The prosperity of the citizens in the 17th century gave rise to the typical "Bergisch" architectural style with its Baroque elements in the three-colour chord of green, white and slate grey. Factory owners and bankers erected the villa district "Brill" at the turn of the century which was not destroyed in the Second World War and attracts many tourists. Although Elberfeld forms the main centre of the city today, Barmen has received a lively, lovable city. Devastating bombing raids on Barmen and Elberfeld in 1943 largely destroyed the inner cities, almost 40% of the building structure in total. Many of the surviving buildings and streets also fell victim to the goal of a "car-friendly" city during reconstruction. It was not until the 1970s that a rethinking in favour of monument protection was able to save the atmosphere of old neighbourhoods. With the exception of Beyenburg, which has retained its village character through the monastery, the other Wuppertal districts have been strongly influenced by the various manifestations of the Protestant, evangelical faith in history. In the past, it was considered to be the city in Germany with the highest proportion of sects, Protestant preponderance has been compensated by the immigration of many people from Catholic regions. Wuppertal is a city of people from many different countries of origin and cultures today.

Numbers

In 1708-9 Elberfeld and Barmen had together about 5,800 inhabitants, in 1863 there were 106,065, by 1900 the number had grown to 360,000. One felt on the way to becoming a half a million city in 1963 as there were 430,000 inhabitants. But the dying German textile industry and the general demographic development led to the population decreasing. Wuppertal had around 351,000 inhabitants in 2016 according to the last count. The highest mountain in the city is the Lichtscheid in the south of Barmen with a height of 350 metres, the lowest point is 100 metres which is measured at the Wupper in Müngsten. The length of the Wupper in the city is 33.9 kilometres, the narrow development of the valley led to an extremely high number of over 100 bridges. Nearly 500 stairways form quick connecting ways for pedestrians between the roads on the steep mountain slopes. Stairways and bridges, the suspension railway scaffolding and many green spaces which are always close to the city characterize the cityscape. "City in the country" used to be an advertising slogan.

University City

The specialised diverse industrial production required good training opportunities. A Latin school was first founded in Elberfeld in 1592 from which the grammar school, secondary school and secondary high school later emerged in the 19th century. The first official school in Barmen was in 1596 as a centre school for the scattered farms. The Higher Commercial School which trained engineers from 1863 on became the Royal United Machine Building School Elberfeld-Barmen in 1987. The Barmen and the Elberfeld Arts and Craft Schools were founded in 1894 and 1897, the Royal Prussian Building Trades School in 1897 for Elberfeld-Barmen and in 1900 the Prussian Higher Technical College for the textile industry in Barmen followed. The Pedagogical Academy Wuppertal was founded in 1946 and has belonged to the Rhineland Educational Colleges since 1965. The Artwork School since 1946, the Institute for Industrial Forms, Industrial Design and the Higher College for the Graphical Industry have become focal points in Wuppertal's vocational training. It is thanks to the initiative of the then NRW Prime Minister, later Federal President Johannes Rau (1931-2006) that a comprehensive university was founded in Wuppertal in 1972 into which these specialist training institutes were integrated. The "Bergisch University" with its campus at Grifflenberg has shaped the cityscape since 2003. The Wuppertal Institute in the building of a former trade school next to the main railway station was founded in 1984 to investigate transformation processes and instruments for sustainable development. Wuppertal became world famous not only for its industrial products, but also as a mission city. A small town in South Africa on the Western Cape which was founded as a mission station in 1832 is called "Wupperthal". The Rhenish Missionary Society was founded in 1828 on the Hardt, the ridge on which the Botanical Garden is located today. Missionaries were trained here and sent to proselytize in the colonies for the evangelical faith. Missionaries brought cult objects of indigenous ethnic groups from there and a remarkable, rich ethnographic collection was created. This can be visited in the "Museum on the Hardt".

A sense of cultural care, enjoyment of opera, theatre and concert life unfolded in the course of the 19th century. The grand, prestigious Historical City Hall in Elberfeld is a testimony to this civic spirit. At the end of the 19th century art lovers in Barmen and Elberfeld founded art collections. The Elberfeld banker August von der Heydt bought the first picture from Picasso that the then promising young painter could sell to a museum in 1908. "Acrobat and young Harlequin" could be seem in Elberfeld, today's Von der Heydt Museum, until 1937. It was confiscated by the National Socialists together with more than 500 pictures and could never return to Wuppertal. But after the war the Wuppertal Heydt Museum was one of the most distinguished museums in West Germany and was able to rebuild very interesting collections. Avant-garde artists found a home in the city. Pina Bausch (1940-2009) and her ensemble thus produced the world-famous, revolutionary choreographies of the Wuppertal Dance Theatre and the British born sculptor Tony Cragg has his studio and his workshops here. His "Waldfried Sculpture Park" has attracted many fans of contemporary art from all over the world. The Museum of Early Industrialization, the Engels House in Barmen and the Bergisch Railway Museums in Kohlfurth on the Wupper show the history of technology and industry. Wuppertal is a place characterized by medium sized industry, as before, with many occupational profiles from the design and creative sectors today. The Nordbahntrasse is a recent attraction. It has been navigating through viaducts, through tunnels and gorges on the track bed of the railway, which used to run past the city to the north, since 2014; the 23 kilometre long Rhenish line has become an attractive, fast cycle path and footpath. Thanks for this route with many great views of the city are due to the "Wupper Movement e.V.", a vigorous, crusading citizens' initiative.

Fußgängerbrücke am Bahnhof Oberbarmen und Wuppertaler Gaskessel in Heckinghausen

Schneckenförmig verlaufen die Wege auf die schwungvolle Fußgängerbrücke aus dem Jahr 1963. Sie verbindet den Ortsteil Heckinghausen mit der Schwebebahnstation und dem Bahnhofsvorplatz von Oberbarmen und führt über die breiten Gleisanlagen, die wiederum die Wupper überbrücken. Von ihr blickt man auf den 66,65 Meter hohen Gaskessel in Heckinghausen. Von 1952-54 errichtete ihn das MAN Werk Gustavsburg über zwanzigeckigem geschweißtem Gussstahlboden mit einem Speichervolumen von 20 000 Kubikmetern. Bis 1997 war er in Betrieb. Eigentlich sollte er abgerissen werden, aber nach heftigen Protesten wurde dieses Heckinghauser Wahrzeichen 1998 unter Denkmalschutz gestellt. Zehn Jahre später, nach umfassenden, auch komplizierten Umbauten, schuf hier ein Investorenteam einen besonderen Erlebnisort mit Restaurant, Fitnessclub und der „Wundermaschine". Der Skywalk auf dem Dach lädt zu einem Rundumblick aus fast 70 Metern Höhe über den Osten Wuppertals ein.

Pedestrian Bridge at Oberbarmen Station and Wuppertal Gas Boiler in Heckinghausen

The spirally formed paths lead to the sweeping pedestrian bridge dating back to 1963. They connect the district of Heckinghausen with the suspension railway station and the station forecourt at Oberbarmen and lead across the wide railway lines which in turn bridge the Wupper. You can look at the 66.65 metre tall gas boiler in Heckinghausen from here. The MAN Gustavsburg plant erected the over twenty-sided welded cast steel floor with a storage volume of 20,000 cubic metres from 1952-54. It was in operation until 1997. It was supposed to be demolished, but this Heckinghausen landmark was placed under a preservation order in 1998 after fierce protests. An investor team created a special experience site with a restaurant, fitness club and the "miracle machine" ten years later after comprehensive as well as complicated conversions. The Skywalk on the roof invites you to take an all-round view over the east of Wuppertal.

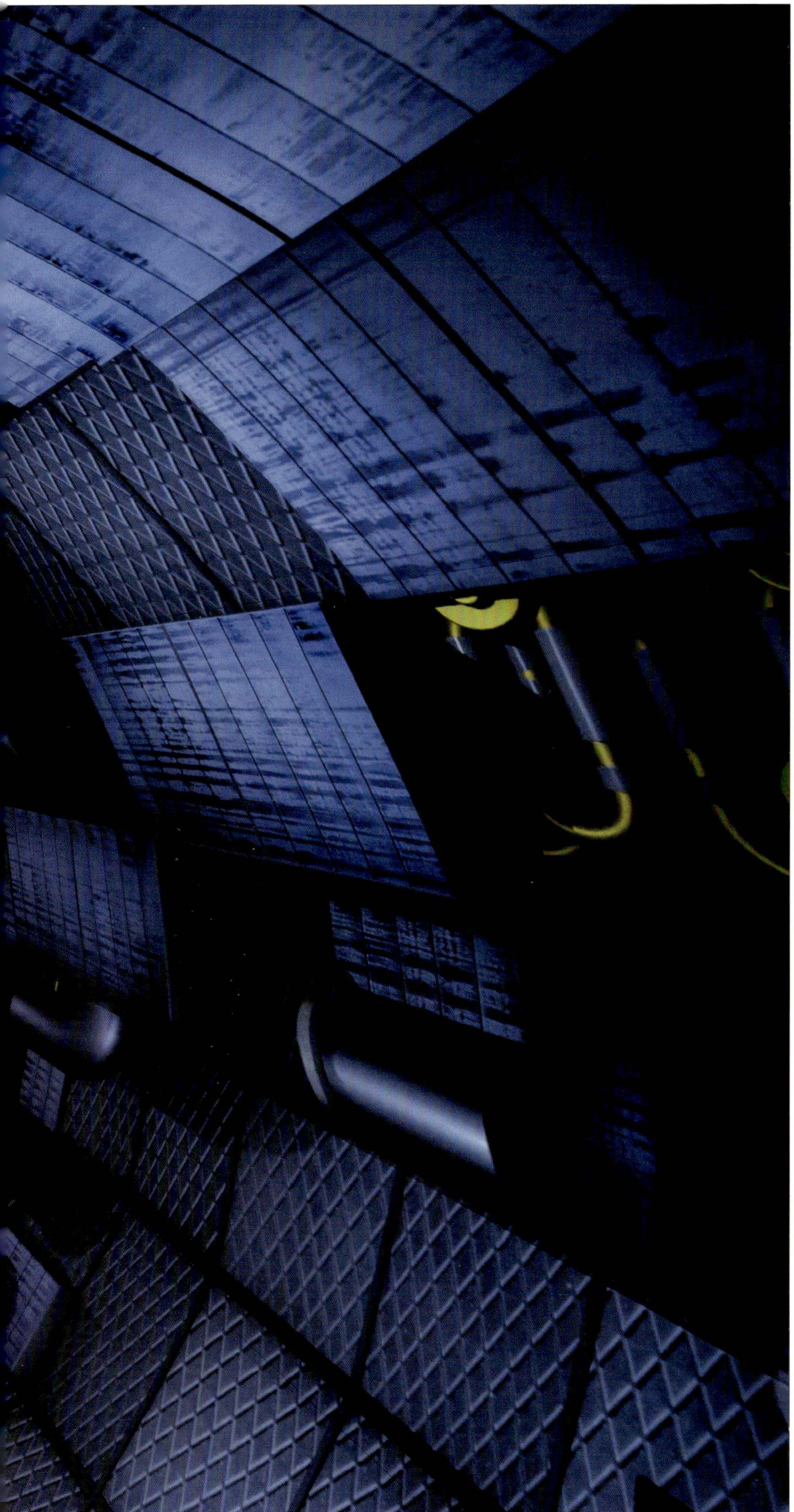

„Wundermaschine" im Wuppertaler Gaskessel in Heckinghausen

Licht- und Farbshows aus 26 Hochleistungsbeamern verwandeln den 47 Meter hohen Innenraum des Kessels in ein 360 Grad Projektionsspektakel. Phantastische, illusionäre Wunderwelten aus Licht und 60 Millionen Pixeln auf einer 6000 Quadratmeter großen Leinwand nehmen die Besucher mit in einen flutenden wie schwerelosen Raum. Das Künstlerkollektiv Urbanscreen, das bereits das Opernhaus Sydneys illuminierte, kreiert hier fantastische Geschichten voller Phantasie. Die „Wundermaschine" ist die erste Lasershow ihrer Art, weitere einzigartige Erlebnisse sind geplant.

"Miracle Machine" in the Wuppertal Gas Boiler in Heckinghausen

Light and colour shows from 26 high-performance beamers transform the 47 metre high interior of the boiler into a 360-degree projection spectacle. Fantastic, illusionary worlds of light and 60 million pixels on a 6,000 square metre screen take visitors into a flooded, weightless-like place. The artist collective Urbanscreen, which has already illuminated the Sydney Opera House, creates fantastic stories full of fantasy here. The "miracle machine" is the first laser show of its kind, further unique experiences are planned.

Altes Fachwerkhaus in der Spieckerstraße 12 a

Dieses liebevoll gepflegte Fachwerkhaus mitten in Heckinghausen wirkt wie ein Kleinod zwischen der Nachkriegsbebauung. Es gehört zu den ältesten erhaltenen Gebäuden der Stadt und wurde 1608 von Hans Heckhaus errichtet. Im Dorf Heckinghausen lebten damals viele Bleicher, die mit dem sanften Wupperwasser in der Wupperaue Garne bleichten. Das alljährliche Bleicherfest erinnert an diese Tradition des alten Stadtteils.

Old Half-timbered House at Spieckerstreet 12 a

This lovingly maintained half-timbered house in the middle of Heckinghausen looks like a gem between the post-war developments. It is one of the oldest surviving buildings in the city and was built by Hans Heckhaus in 1608. Many bleachers who bleached yarn with the gentle Wupper water on the river meadows lived in the village of Heckinghausen at that time. The annual bleacher festival serves as a reminder of this tradition of the old district.

Heckinghauser Zollbrücke

Die älteste erhaltene Brücke Wuppertals verbindet seit 1775 das Rauental und die Bockmühle im Osten Heckinghausens. Wer am Zollhaus auf der Brückenmitte vorbeikam, hatte die Grenze zwischen der preußischen Grafschaft Mark und dem Herzogtum Berg überschritten. „Über die Wupper gehen" sagt man in Wuppertal, wenn jemand stirbt, oder wenn eine Firma Konkurs anmelden muss. Es gibt aber auch eine positive Bedeutung der Redewendung: Die Wupper bildete die Grenze zwischen Berg und Mark. Wer im 18. Jahrhundert zum Beispiel aus Schwelm über die Wupper kam, war vor dem preußischen Militärdienst sicher.

Heckinghausen Toll Bridge

The oldest preserved bridge in Wuppertal has connected Rauental and Bockmühle in the east of Heckinghausen since 1775. Anyone passing the toll house in the middle of the bridge had crossed the border between the Prussian County of Mark and the Duchy of Berg. "Go over the Wupper" is said in Wuppertal if someone dies or if a company has to declare bankruptcy. But the expression also has a positive meaning: The Wupper formed the border between Berg and Mark. Anyone who crossed the River Wupper from Schwelm in the 18th century was safe from Prussian military service, for example.

626 Radevormwald
WSW mobil
616

Wendehalle und Schwebebahnstation Oberbarmen

Das größte, längste Bauwerk der Stadt ist zugleich ihr Wahrzeichen, die Schwebebahn. Fast 30 Jahre vor der Vereinigung der Städte Elberfeld und Barmen einigten sich die Bürger auf das gemeinsame, pionierhafte Verkehrsmittel. Das 13,3 Kilometer lange Stahlgerüst von Oberbarmen bis Vohwinkel wurde von 1898 bis 1903 über dem Bett der Wupper errichtet und löste geradezu genial alle Verkehrsprobleme im Tal. Von 1998 bis 2008 wurden ihr Gerüst und die Bahnhöfe erneuert. Die Oberbarmer Wendehalle wurde vergrößert. Die blauen schnittigen Wagen fahren seit 2019, werktags im Zweiminutentakt, und befördern täglich an die 82 000 Fahrgäste. Da es in der langen Geschichte nur zwei Unfälle gab, gilt sie immer noch als sicherstes Verkehrsmittel der Welt.

Oberbarmen Suspension Railway Station with Turning Hall

The largest, longest construction in the city is also its landmark, the suspension railway. The citizens agreed on the common, pioneering means of transport almost 30 years before the unification of the cities of Elberfeld and Barmen. The 13.3 kilometre long steel framework from Oberbarmen Barmen to Vohwinkel was built from 1898 to 1903 over the bed of the Wupper and ingeniously solved almost all the traffic problems in the valley. The scaffolding and stations were renewed from 1998 to 2008. The Oberbarmen turning hall was enlarged. The sleek blue hanging cars have been operating every two minutes on weekdays since 2019, carrying around 82,000 passengers every day. It is still considered the safest means of transport in the world as there have only been two accidents in its long history.

Fachwerkhaus Eylauer Straße 15

Das schön restaurierte Fachwerkhaus mit seiner Freitreppe an der Eylauer Straße 15 in Wichlinghausen entstand um 1780. Es gehört zum alten Ortskern, dem „Dorp" Wichelkusen. Westfälische Siedler haben wahrscheinlich hier im 9.Jahrhundert gesiedelt. Darauf weist die Namensendung „inghausen", wie auch in Heckinghausen, hin. Wichlinghausen entstand so aus „Wichmaringhusen". Der Ort im Norden von Barmen hat noch viele idyllische Ecken, auch wenn hier im 19. Jahrhundert große Bandfabriken errichtet wurden.

Half-Timbered House at Eylauer Street 15

The beautifully restored half-timbered house with its outside staircase at Eylauer Street 15 in Wichlinghausen was built around 1780. It belongs to the old town centre, the "Dorp" Wichelkusen. Westphalian settlers probably settled here in the 9th century. This is indicated by the name ending "inghausen", as in Heckinghausen. Wichlinghausen originated from "Wichmaringhusen". The village in the north of Barmen still has many idyllic corners even though large textile factories were built here in the 19th century.

Gottesbrünnlein

Eine kleine Parkanlage beim Wichlinghauser Markt hat als Zentrum das „Gottesbrünnlein". Von 1780-85 entstand die gemauerte Brunnenfassung einer Quelle. Sie wurde später mit einem Tor verschlossen. Bei ihrer Restaurierung im Jahr 1975 erhielt es die stufenweise Einfassung. Über ihr wurde der alte Brunnenspruch wieder angebracht: „Gottes Brune / ein het Wass / er die Fulle / Anno 1781". Heute allerdings ist der Brunnen an die städtische Wasserleitung angeschlossen. Die Gedenktafel an der Mauereinfassung erinnert an den Ehrenbürger Dr. Klaus Brauda (1901-1970), der CDU-Mitbegründer, Bürgermeister in Wuppertal und Mitglied des Landtags war und sich 1953 für den Sozialen Wohnungsbau eingesetzt hat.

God`s Well

The small park at Wichlinghausen market has the "God`s Well" as its centre. The masonry well socket of a spring was created from 1780-85. It was later closed with a door. It received the surrounding steps during its restoration in 1975. The old fountain sayings were reinstalled over it: "Gottes Brune / ein het Wass / er die Fulle / Anno 1781". The well is connected to the municipal water supply today, however. The commemorative plaque on the perimeter wall commemorates honorary citizen Dr. Klaus Brauda (1901-1970), the CDU co-founder, mayor in Wuppertal and a member of the state parliament, who spoke up for social housing in 1953..

Villa Halstenbach

Die „Villa Halstenbach" in der Straße Am Diek 47, Baudenkmal seit 1980, spiegelt den Baustil in der zweiten Hälfte des 19. Jahrhunderts. Repräsentation sollte mit heimatbezogenen, älteren Bauelementen wie dem Fachwerk im Schaugiebel eine Verbindung eingehen. Dazu gehört das weit ausladende Satteldach, der herausspringende Mittelrisalit für den Windfang und Erker im Obergeschoss. 1922 erwarb Willy Halstenbach (1886-1953), Inhaber einer Gummiband- und Maschinenfabrik, das Gebäude. In seinem Haus, das nach dem 2. Weltkrieg eine Keimzelle der CDU wurde, trafen sich während nationalsozialistischer Zeit im Geheimen Vertreter der Bekennenden Kirche wie Martin Niemöller und Hanns Lilje. Im Gärtnerhäuschen der Villa erhielten der spätere NRW-Ministerpräsident Johannes Rau und Kurt Drees Privatunterricht.

Halstenbach Villa

"Villa Halstenbach" located at Am Diek 47, a protected building since 1980, reflects the architectural style in the second half of the 19th century. Representation should connect with home-related, older components such as the framework in the windowed gables. These include the wide sweeping saddle roof, the projecting middle for the vestibule and bay windows on the upper floor. In 1922 Willy Halstenbach (1886-1953), owner of a rubber band and machine factory, acquired the building. Representatives of the Confessing Church such as Martin Niemöller and Hanns Lilje met in secret during the National Socialist era in this house which became a nucleus of the CDU after World War II. Johannes Rau, later NRW Prime Minister, and Kurt Drees received private lessons in the gardener`s cottage of the villa.

Skywalk im Nordpark

Liebhaber von Sonnenaufgängen haben seit 2017 im Nordpark eine fantastische Aussichtsplattform bekommen; aber auch die anderen Besucher des Nordparks freuen sich über den neuen, weiten Blick auf Barmen. Der „Skywalk" beim Ehrenhain ragt mit seinem 16,50 Meter langen Aussichtssteg aus dem Wald heraus und endet in einer elliptischen Plattform, auf der in 6,50 Meter Höhe das Gefühl vermittelt wird zu schweben. Dieser neue Aussichtsplatz entstand während der grundlegenden Erneuerung des Parks von 2009-2018. Gut 30 Jahre nach den Barmer Anlagen wurde er 1895 durch Initiative des Nordstädter Bürgervereins für die Bürger Wichlinghausens eingerichtet.

Skywalk in North Park

Those who love sunrises have had a fantastic viewing platform in North Park since 2017; but the other visitors to North Park are also pleased with the new, broad view of Barmen. The "Skywalk" at Ehrenhain rises out of the forest with its 16.50 metre long lookout platform and ends in an elliptical platform on which the feeling of floating is conveyed at a height of 6.50 metres. This new observation site was created during the fundamental renovation of the park from 2009-2018. It was established for the citizens of Wichlinghausen in 1895 through the initiative of the Nordstadt Civic Association, a good 30 years after the Barmen grounds.

Turmterrassen im Nordpark

Zum Gelände des Nordparks gehörte auch das frühere Gut des Fabrikanten Hugo Greeff (1830-1906), auf dem Bauernhof und ein Landhaus ein Ensemble bildeten. Das Landhaus wurde 1897 zum Parkrestaurant, im ehemaligen Obsthof entstand der Biergarten. 1904 stockte man den Erker zum Turm auf, das Restaurant erhielt den Namen „Turmterrassen". Bis 1970 war das Ausflugsrestaurant geöffnet. Erst 2009 verkaufte die Stadt das marode Gebäude, das nach der sorgfältigen Restaurierung Gästen wieder abwechslungsreiche Tapasvariationen aus regionalen Produkten bietet.

Turmterrassen in North Park

The grounds of North Park also included the former estate of the manufacturer Hugo Greeff (1830-1906) on which the farm and a country house formed an ensemble. The country house became a park restaurant in 1897 and the beer garden was created in the former orchard. The oriel was increased to a tower in 1904, the restaurant was named "Turmterrassen" ("tower terrace"). The excursion restaurant was open until 1970. The city first sold the dilapidated building in 2009, which after careful restoration offers guests diverse tapas variations made from regional products.

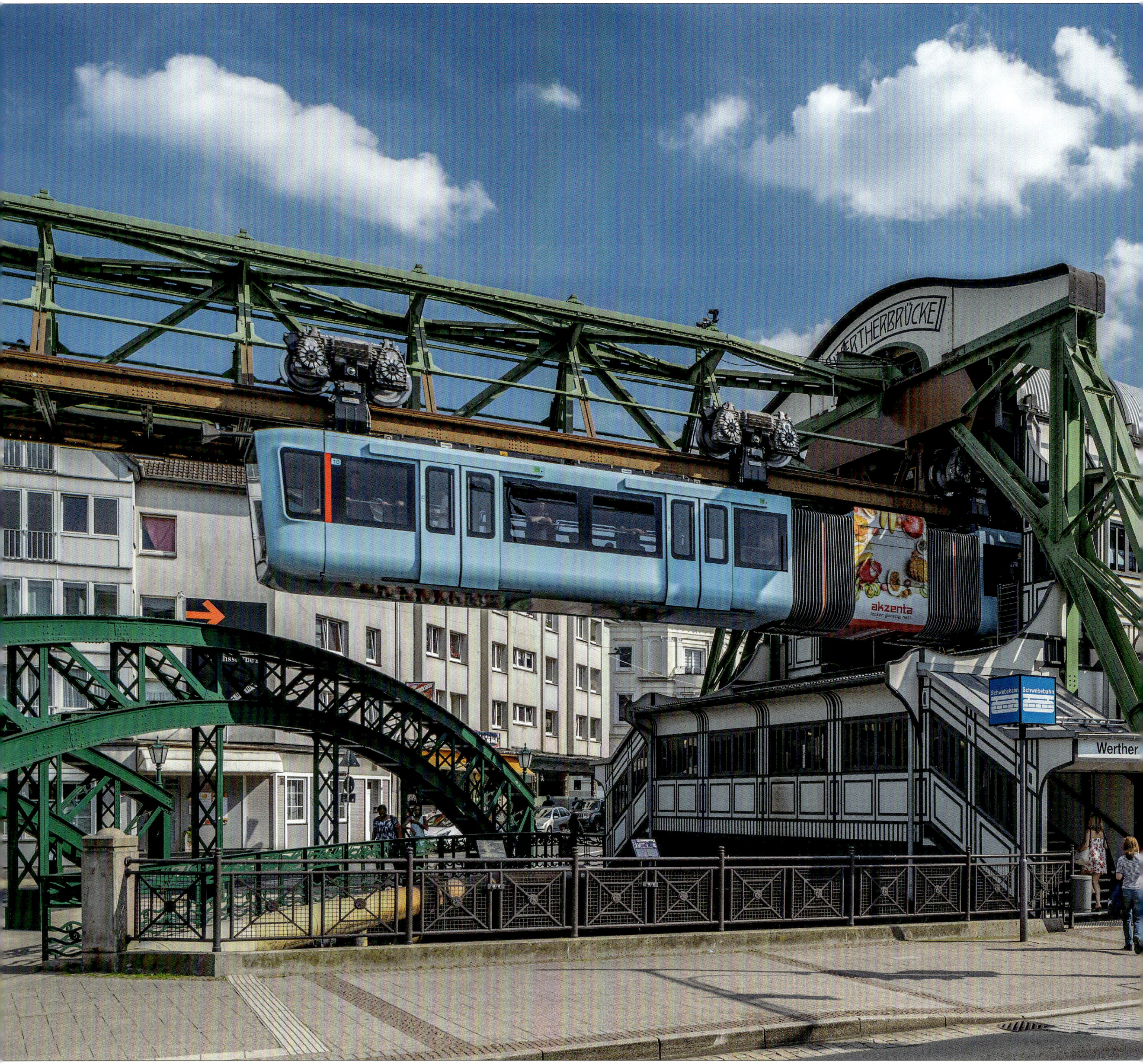
ERTHERBRÜCKE
akzenta
Schwebebahn
Schwebebahn
Werther

Werther Brücke

Linearer Jugendstil und sachliche Stahlkonstruktion gehen in diesem 1903 errichteten Bahnhof eine geglückte Synthese ein. Der bergische Farbdreiklang aus dem Schwarz und Weiß der Bahnhofswände und dem Grün des Stahlgerüsts prägen dieses Brückenviertel. Bei der Erneuerung des Schwebebahngerüsts verhinderten der Bergische Geschichtsverein und eine aktive Bürgerinitiative den Abriss. Der Bahnhof Werther Brücke und die beiden Stationen Landgericht und Völklinger Straße wurden „formidentisch" rekonstruiert. Alle Schwebebahnhöfe haben heute auch Fahrstühle.

Werther Bridge

Linear Art Nouveau and factual steel construction enter into a successful synthesis in this station built in 1903. The Bergisch colour triad of the black and white of the station walls and the green of the steel framework characterize this bridge district. The Bergisch history society and an active citizens' initiative prevented the demolition during the renewal of the suspension railway structure. The station Werther Brücke and the two stations Landgericht (district court) and Völklinger Street were reconstructed in the same way. All the suspended railway stations also have elevators today.

Office4U
AYK
reisen
anastasio
JORDAN

Werther Brunnen und Husch Husch

Den Eingang der Barmer Flanier- und Einkaufsmeile „Werth" markiert der große Brunnen. Der in Barmen geborene Düsseldorfer Bildhauer Friedrich Werthmann (1927-2018) stellte ihn als zwei Halbkugeln dar. Wasser aus mehreren Düsen lässt im spannungsvollen Raum zwischen ihnen ein reizvolles Spiel aus Licht und Wasser entstehen. Die Doppelkugel bezeichnet als „Sonne" den Wuppertaler „Astropfad". Lehrer und Schüler des 1579 gegründeten Barmer Gymnasiums Sedanstraße schufen entlang der Talachse ein erwanderbares Modell des Sonnensystems. Maßstabgerecht finden sich in der Stadt Bronzetafeln für die Planeten. Die Erde liegt noch auf dem Werth (Ecke Kleine Flurstraße), die Tafel für Pluto schließlich an der Endstation der Schwebebahn in Vohwinkel.

In den 1920er und 1930er Jahren war der Hausierer Peter Held (1886-1953) stadtbekannt. Wenn er von den Kindern mit „Husch-Husch" angerufen wurde, konnte er sehr wütend und jähzornig werden. Die Kinder machten sich einen bösen Spaß daraus zu rufen und wegzulaufen. Wie in der Elberfelder City die Figuren von „Mina Knallenfalls" und „Zuckerfritz" an Originale der Stadt erinnern, wurde 2004 auf Grund von Bürgerinitiativen die Figur des „Husch-Husch" im Werth nach dem Entwurf des Wuppertaler Bildhauers Klaus Buhrandt aufgestellt. Peter Held war ein äußerst unangepasster Mensch, der während des Nationalsozialismus auch Zuchthaushaft ertragen musste.

Werther Fountain and Husch Husch

The large fountain highlights the entrance to the Barmen strolling and shopping mile "Werth". Barmen-born Düsseldorf sculptor Friedrich Werthmann (1927-2018) presented it as two hemispheres. Water from several jets creates a delightful play of light and water in the exciting space between them. The double ball called Sonne (sun) is the start of the Wuppertal Astropfad (astro path). Teachers and students of the Barmen Sedanstraße Grammar School, founded in 1579, created an alterable model of the solar system along the Wupper valley. True to scale bronze plates for the planets can be found in the city. The earth is still on the Werth (corner of Kleine Flurstraße), the plaque for Pluto is at the terminus of the suspension railway in Vohwinkel.

The peddler Peter Held (1886-1953) was known in the city in the 1920s and 1930s. He could become very angry and irascible when he was called "Husch-Husch" by the children. The children had wicked fun calling to him and running away. The figure of "Husch-Husch" was established in 2004, according to the design of the Wuppertal sculptor Klaus Buhrandt, on the basis of citizens' initiatives, just as the figures of "Mina Knallenfalls" and "Zuckerfritz" in Elberfeld serve as a reminder of originals of the city. Peter Held was an extremely nonconformist person who had to endure imprisonment during National Socialism.

Wuppertaler Brauhaus

Eines der ältesten Hallenbäder Deutschlands errichtete 1881-1882 die Stadt Barmen neben dem Rathaus an der „Kleinen Flurstraße". Als Baudenkmal erhielt es Schutz vor Abriss im Jahr 1988; fünf Jahre später wurde es geschlossen, weil es nicht mehr rentabel wirtschaften konnte. Aber 1997 eröffnete in dem schönen Gebäude mit seinen Rundbögen, den Natursteinsäulen, den flachen Zeltdächern und der polygonen Apsis, in der sich früher das Schwimmbecken der Frauen befand, das beliebte „Wuppertaler Brauhaus" mit der einzigen Brauerei der Stadt. Im ehemaligen Herrenbecken des Schwimmbads befindet sich die „größte Theke Wuppertals".

Wuppertal Brewery

The city of Barmen built one of the oldest indoor swimming pools in Germany next to the town hall on "Kleine Flurstraße" in 1881-1882. It received protection from demolition in 1988 as a listed building, but was closed five years later because it was no longer profitable. But in 1997 the popular "Wuppertaler Brauhaus", the only brewery in the city, opened in the beautiful building with its round arches, natural stone pillars, flat tent roofs and the polygonal apse, which was once the women's swimming pool. The "largest bar in Wuppertal" is to be found in the former men's pool of the swimming pool.

wuppertaler brauhaus
wupper hell
WUPPERTALER
BRAUHAUS

Alter Markt, Schwebebahnstation und Fischtreppe

Vier mächtige, 38 Meter hohe Stahlpylonen halten die Seile der Gerüstbrücke für die Wuppertaler Schwebebahn an der Station „Alter Markt". Diese aufwändige Konstruktion aus dem Jahr 1967 überspannt den Verkehrsknotenpunkt im Zentrum Barmens über 120 Meter Länge und machte den Ausbau der Talachse möglich, über die die Bundesstraße 7 vier- bis siebenspurig geführt wird. Die zwei tragenden Pylonen für die Stahlseile der Brücke sind 38 Meter hoch. Nichts erinnert an diesem riesenhaften, weiten Verkehrsknotenpunkt an den dicht bebauten Alten Markt vor dem 2. Weltkrieg.

Seit 1993 hat der Wupperverband die Wupper von der Mündung in Leverkusen bis Wuppertal-Beyenburg und weiter bis Hückeswagen und auch einen Teil ihrer Nebenflüsse an Wehren und Staustufen für Wanderfische wieder durchlässig gemacht. Dazu gehören Fischtreppen, die den Fischen die Möglichkeit geben, im Fluss aufzusteigen. Der Fischaufstieg in der Wupper beim Alten Markt ist auch eine Maßnahme zur teilweisen Renaturierung des Flussbetts und seiner Ufer, denn im Zuge der Industrialisierung wurde die Wupper im 19. Jahrhundert von der Industrie als Abwasserkanal genutzt.

Alter Markt, Suspension Railway Station and Fish Ladders

Four mighty, 38 metre high steel pylons hold the cables of the scaffolding bridge for the Wuppertal suspension railway at the Alter Markt (old market) station. This elaborate construction from 1967 spans the traffic hub in the centre of Barmen over a length of 120 meters and made the expansion of the valley axis possible, over which the federal highway 7 is structured in four to seven lanes. The two supporting pylons for the steel cables of the bridge are also 38 metres high. No part of this huge, wide traffic junction is reminiscent of the densely built old market before the Second World War.

The Wupper Association has been making the Wupper permeable once more for migratory fish, from the mouth in Leverkusen to Wuppertal-Beyenburg and on to Hückeswagen and also to a part of their tributaries on weirs and barrages since 1993. The fish ladders that give fish the opportunity to ascend the river belong thereto. The fish ascent in the Wupper at the old market is also a measure for the partial renaturation of the riverbed and its shores because in the course of industrialization the Wupper was used as a sewer in the 19th century.

„I am alive", Skulptur von Tony Cragg

Wie eine spiegelnde Feder bäumt sich die Edelstahl-Skulptur von Tony Cragg auf dem Grünstreifen vor dem Opernhaus auf, sprühend vor Energie und Lebensfreude. Der in Wuppertal lebende, weltberühmte Bildhauer Tony Cragg, 1949 in Liverpool geboren, hat dieses „Lebenszeichen" geschaffen, eine unvergessliche Form, die allen, die am Opernhaus vorüberfahren, im Gedächtnis bleibt. Der frühere Rektor der Kunstakademie Düsseldorf eröffnete 2008 den Skulpturenpark in Unterbarmen, einen Publikumsmagneten für Kunstfreunde aus der ganzen Welt.

"I am alive", Sculpture by Tony Cragg

The stainless steel sculpture by Tony Cragg rears up like a reflective feather on the green strip in front of the opera house, sparkling with energy and a love of life. The world-famous sculptor Tony Cragg, a resident of Wuppertal, who was born in Liverpool in 1949, has created this "sign of life", an unforgettable shape that stays in the memory of everyone who passes by the opera house. The former headmaster of the Düsseldorf Art Academy opened the sculpture park in Unterbarmen in 2008, a magnet for art lovers from all over the world.

Barmer Bahnhof

Wie einen griechischen Tempel erbaute 1911 die Stadt Barmen ihren Hauptbahnhof. Das frühere Gebäude der Bergisch-Märkischen Eisenbahngesellschaft aus dem Jahr 1847 war wegen Verbreiterung der Gleise abgebrochen worden. Elf Jahre nach Elberfeld, wo die älteste Westdeutsche Eisenbahngesellschaft gegründet worden war, schloss sich auch Barmen mit der Bergisch-Märkischen Eisenbahngesellschaft an das Schienennetz an. Von Elberfeld aus fuhren Personen- und Güterzüge nach Barmen, Schwelm und seit dem Frühjahr 1848 weiter nach Dortmund. Eine Strecke nach Remscheid wurde erst 1868 eröffnet. Parallel zur Bergisch-Märkischen Bahn im Tal konnte 1879 die Strecke im Norden Barmens über Wichlinghausen nach Hagen bis Dortmund ihren Betrieb aufnehmen.
Der Barmer Bahnhof verlor seine Bedeutung als Hauptbahnhof nach 1929, als Barmen und Elberfeld sich zu Wuppertal zusammenschlossen. Heute ist das Gebäude ein besonderes Event-Lokal. Ein Besuch in der Bahnhofsbuchhandlung macht alle Opernfreunde glücklich, denn der berühmte Opernbass Kurt Rydl wurde 2008 Eigentümer des Bahnhofs mit Buchhandlung und Café. Über Lautsprecher eingespielt geben seine Arien der Bahnhofshalle eine beschwingte Stimmung.

Barmen Station

The city of Barmen built its central station like a Greek temple in 1911. The former building of the Bergisch-Märkisch railway company from 1847 had been demolished because of widening of the tracks. Barmen also joined the rail network with the Bergisch-Märkisch railway company eleven years after Elberfeld where the oldest West German railway company had been founded. Passengers and freight trains went from Elberfeld to Barmen, Schwelm and on to Dortmund from the spring of 1848 on. A route to Remscheid was first opened in 1868. The line in the north of Barmen via Wichlinghausen to Hagen and Dortmund began operation in 1879 at the same time as the Bergisch-Märkisch railway in the valley.
Barmen station lost its importance as a main station after 1929, when Barmen and Elberfeld joined together with Wuppertal. The building is a special event venue today. A visit to the station bookstore makes all opera friends happy because the famous opera bass Kurt Rydl became the owner of the station with bookstore and café in 2008. His arias, played over loudspeakers, provide the station concourse with a lively atmosphere.

Engelsgarten

Gleich neben dem Opernhaus öffnet sich der weite Engelsgarten, der seinen Namen von der Fabrikantenfamilie des Begründers des Wissenschaftlichen Sozialismus Friedrich Engels (1820-1895) hat. Er veröffentlichte gemeinsam mit Karl Marx 1848 „Das Kommunistische Manifest" und leitete damit gesellschaftliche Reformprozesse ein. An die prächtigen Barockbauten hier in der Talaue des weiten Wupperbogens erinnert noch das „Engelshaus", in dem sich heute das „Historische Zentrum" der Stadt befindet. An das im 2. Weltkrieg zerstörte Geburtshaus des berühmten Reformers erinnert an der Ostseite des Gartens ein Gedenkstein. Gegenüber dem Engelshaus steht die mächtige Skulptur „Die starke Linke" aus einem weißen Marmorblock, die der österreichische Bildhauer Alfred Hrdlicka (1928-2009) schuf. Die Ketten sprengende Kraft der Arbeiterbewegung fand hier einprägsame Form.

Engels Garden

The wide Engels garden which derived its name from the manufacturing family of the founder of scientific Socialism Friedrich Engels (1820-1895) opens up right next to the Opera House He jointly published "The Communist Manifesto" with Karl Marx in 1848 and thus led a social reform process. The Engelshaus which today accommodates the city's "Historic Centre" serves as a reminder of the splendid Baroque buildings here in the valley of the wide Wupper Curve, just as a memorial stone on the eastern side of the garden, which was destroyed in World War II, does of the birthplace of the famous reformer. The mighty sculpture "The Strong Left" made of a white marble block, created by the Austrian sculptor Alfred Hrdlicka (1928-2009), is located opposite the Engels House. The immense force of the labour movement found memorable form here.

Engelsstatue im Engelsgarten

Der Engelsgarten war öfters ein Ort herausragender politischer Ereignisse. So wurde im September 1987, zwei Jahre vor der „Wende", extra eine Straße für den Besuch des damaligen Staatspräsidenten Erich Honecker im Engelshaus über die B 7 gelegt. Der Sänger und Schlagzeuger Udo Lindenberg schenkte ihm spektakulär eine Gitarre. Am 28. November 2011 besuchte Ma Kai, stellvertretender Ministerpräsident der Volksrepublik China, das Engelshaus. Als Gastgeschenk brachte er bei dieser Gelegenheit eine monumentale Bronzestatue von Friedrich Engels mit, die seit 2014 von einem Pyramidenstumpf aus 3,85 Meter Höhe väterlich und nachdenklich auf die Menschen im Park herabblickt. Im Stil eines moderneren, sozialistischen Realismus schuf sie der Direktor des staatlichen Chinesischen Skulptureninstituts Zeng Chenggang. „Die Arbeit ist die Quelle allen Reichtums..." steht am Anfang eines langen Zitats aus den Schriften Friedrich Engels auf ihrem Sockel.

Engels Statue in Engels Garden

The Engelsgarten was often a place of outstanding political events. An extra street was thus placed over the B 7 for the visit of the former GDR-President Erich Honecker in the Engels House in September 1987, two years before "reunification". The singer and drummer Udo Lindenberg gave him a spectacular guitar. Ma Kai, Deputy Prime Minister of the People's Republic of China, visited the Engels House on November 28, 2011. He brought a monumental bronze statue of Friedrich Engels with him as a gift on this occasion that has looked down on the people in the park in a fatherly and thoughtful way from a truncated pyramid at a height of 3.85 metres since 2014. Zeng Chenggang, the director of the State Chinese Sculpture Institute, created it in the style of a more modern, socialist realism. "Work is the source of all wealth ..." is the beginning of a long quotation from the writings of Friedrich Engels on its pedestal.

Museum für Frühindustrialisierung

1970 eröffnete im Patrizierhaus aus dem Jahr 1774 am Westrand des Engelsgartens das Museum für Frühindustrialisierung. Der Biographie Friedrich Engels und der Geschichte seiner Familie ist die Ausstellung in der schönen Barockvilla gewidmet. Die Geschichte der Industrialisierung Wuppertals und vor allem auch der wirtschaftlichen und sozialen Strukturen im „Manchestertum" des 19. Jahrhunderts findet sich in dem alten Fabrikgebäude in Backsteinbauweise der Kannegießer'schen Fabrik hinter dem „Engelshaus". Im Jahr 2018 wegen umfassender Restaurierung und Neukonzeption geschlossen, ist das Museum 2020, im Jahr des 200. Geburtstage Friedrich Engels, wieder eröffnet.

Early Industrialisation Museum

The museum for early industrialization opened in 1970 in the patrician house, which is from 1774, on the western edge of the Engels Garden. The exhibition in the beautiful baroque villa is dedicated to the biography of Friedrich Engels and the story of his family. The history of the industrialization of Wuppertal and above all of the economic and social structures in 19th century "Manchesterism" can be found in the old factory building, in traditional brick style, of the Kannegießer factory behind the Engelshaus. Closed in 2018 due to extensive restoration and redesign the museum reopened in 2020, the year of the 200th anniversary of Friedrich Engels.

Theater am Engelsgarten

Drei große Inszenierungen in der Spielzeit finden auf der Bühne des Opernhauses statt. 2013 schloss die Stadt das erst 1966 eröffnete große Schauspielhaus an der Kluse, weil seine Instandsetzung nicht mehr zu finanzieren war. Schauspiele wurden danach auch im Barmer Opernhaus inszeniert. Da das Sprechtheater jedoch nicht mehr so starkes Publikumsinteresse fand, entschloss man sich zum Bau eines kleinen Theaters für Kammerspiele im Hof des Museums für Frühindustrialisierung. Am 27. September eröffnete das schlichte neue Spielhaus für 160 Zuschauer mit einem eigenen Ensemble. Die Aufführungen werden sehr gut besucht.

Theatre at Engels Garden

The city closed the large theatre on the Kluse, which had only opened in 1966, in 2013 because its repairs could no longer be financed. Plays were also staged at the Barmen Opera House after that. The decision was made to build a smaller venue for intimate performances in the courtyard of the Early Industrialisation Museum as the spoken theatre no longer attracted such strong public interest. The simple new playhouse opened for 160 spectators with its own ensemble on September 27. The performances are very well attended. Three major productions per season take place on the stage of the opera house.

Opernhaus

Ende des 19. Jahrhunderts wollten sich auch die Barmer Bürger aktiv für Kultur und Bildung einsetzen. Ihr Selbstbewusstsein spiegelte 1874 der Bau des ersten Stadttheaters, damals an der Straße „Fischertal". Von der Kanzel der puristischen Reformierten Kirche wurde es allerdings verteufelt, und als es schon ein Jahr später durch einen Heizungsschaden abbrannte, fühlten sich die „Frommen" in der Stadt bestätigt. In einem Jahr wiederaufgebaut zog auch die große Oper in Barmen ein. 1902 wurde es nach einem Brand in einem Jugendstil-Neubau, nun am heutigen Standort (Neuer Weg), eröffnet. Der Bombenangriff auf Barmen am 30. Mai 1943 zerstörte auch das Stadttheater. Erst 1949 erhielt das Gebäude durch Spendenmittel ein provisorisches Dach, und im Oktober 1956 konnte es nun als Wuppertaler Opernhaus wieder eröffnet werden. Nach mehrjähriger umfassender Restaurierung ist es heute ein großartiges Beispiel neoklassizistischer Architektur der Nachkriegszeit.

Opera House

The citizens of Barmen also wanted to actively promote culture and education at the end of the 19th century. Their self-confidence reflected the construction of the first city theatre in 1874, at that time on Fischertal Street. It was demonized by the pulpit of the Purist Reformed Church, however, and the "pious" in the city felt verified when it burned down a year later due to heating damage. Rebuilt in a year, the big opera in Barmen moved in as well. It was opened at its present location (Neuer Weg) in 1902, after a fire in a new art nouveau construction. The bombing of Barmen on May 30, 1943 also destroyed the city theatre. It was not until 1949 that the building received a provisional roof, due to donations, and in October 1956 it was reopened as the Wuppertal Opera House. Today it is a great example of post-war neoclassical architecture after several years of extensive restoration.

Tanztheater Pina Bausch

Ein Höhepunkt in der großartigen Theatergeschichte Wuppertals begann Anfang der 1970er Jahre, als Intendant Arno Wüstenhöfer die junge Choreographin Pina Bausch (1940-2009) zur Ballettdirektorin machte. Mit ihr zog ein revolutionärer neuer Tanzstil ein, der in der ganzen Welt Schule machte, in Wuppertal allerdings lange Zeit viele Besucher zum lauten Türenknallen beim Herauslaufen aus den faszinierenden Vorstellungen veranlasste. Pina Bausch und ihr Tanztheater Wuppertal hielten unbeirrbar durch. Hier wurde Tanzgeschichte gemacht: das Ballett befreite sich aus der bloßen Funktion als Opernbeiwerk. Pina Bausch schuf eine neue, die Menschen tief ergreifende Tanzsprache. Auch nach Pina Bauschs Tod arbeitet das Tanztheater weiter in der ganzen Welt und in mehreren Zeitabschnitten auch im Wuppertaler Opernhaus.

Dance Theatre Pina Bausch

A highlight of Wuppertal's great theatre history started at the beginning of the 1970s when director Arno Wüstenhöfer made the young choreographer Pina Bausch (1940-2009) the ballet director. She introduced a revolutionary new dance style which was performed by schools all over the world, but caused many visitors to feel compelled to slam the doors loudly when walking out of the fascinating performance in Wuppertal. Pina Bausch and her Tanztheater Wuppertal held on unwaveringly. Dance history was made here: the ballet freed itself from the mere function as an opera accessory. Pina Bausch created a new, deeply moving dance language. The dance theatre continues to work throughout the world and in the Wuppertal Opera House for numerous periods of time even after Pina Bausch's death.

Kuhler Viadukt

Heute empfindet man es fast als rücksichtslos, wie radikal pragmatisch der Streckenverlauf der Rheinischen Strecke durch die Wohnorte Barmens und Elberfelds gelegt wurde. Sehr wenig Abstand hatten die Züge zu den an den Hang gebauten Mietshäusern. Die vier hohen, zum Teil mehrbogigen Viadukte in Backsteinbauweise geben den Wohnvierteln eine ganz eigene Atmosphäre. Sechs Viadukte hat die Strecke insgesamt, allein 19 Bögen das 280 Meter lange Viadukt über den Steinweg am Alten Markt und weiter über die Straßen am Rott mit einer Bogenhöhe bis zu 20 Metern. Für die Fahrradfahrer auf der Nordbahntrasse bilden sich überraschende Blicke auf die Stadt.

Kuhler Viaduct

How radically pragmatic the track layout of the Rhenish route was through the homes of Barmen and Elberfeld is seen as almost reckless today. The trains had very little distance to the apartment blocks built on the hillside and the four high brick viaducts, sometimes with numerous arches, give the residential areas a very unique atmosphere. The route has six viaducts. The 280 metre long viaduct over Steinweg on the Alter Markt has 9 arches alone and an arch height of up to 20 metres farther across the roads on the Rott. Cyclists on the Nordbahntrasse are offered surprising views of the city.

St. Antonius

Die „Muttergemeinde" aller Barmer katholischen Gemeinden errichtete 1708 im Zentrum Barmens ihre erste Kirche. Im zweiten Weltkrieg wurde der dritte Nachfolgebau beim Bombenangriff in der Nacht vom 30. Mai 1943 zerstört. Nur der hohe Backsteinturm blieb in den unteren Geschossen erhalten. 1969 wurde der Grundstein für einen außerordentlichen neuen Kirchenbau in der Architektursprache des 20. Jahrhunderts gelegt. Backstein im Turm der Vorgängerkirche in der Verbindung mit zeitgenössischem Beton und Glas prägen die neue, neben dem Turm wie aufgefaltet wirkende Halle. Der Aachener Architekt Professor Horst Kohl machte die Pläne. 1973 wurde die Kirche durch Kardinal Joseph Höffner geweiht. Sie bietet 500 Sitzplätze und kann mehr als 2500 Personen fassen. Ihre Orgel aus dem Jahr 1973 schuf der Bonner Orgelbauer Klais. Das Geläut der Vorgängerkirche mit 5 Bronzeglocken wurde übernommen.

St. Antonius

The "mother community" of all Barmen Catholic communities built their first church in 1708 in the centre of Barmen. The third successor was destroyed in the Second World War during the bombing on the night of May 30, 1943. Only the high brick tower was preserved on the lower floors. The foundation stone was laid for an extraordinary new church in 1969 in the architectural dialogue of the 20th century. Brick in the tower of the previous church in combination with contemporary concrete and glass characterise the hall with its tent- like unfolded effect next to the tower. The Aachen architect Professor Horst Kohl made the plans. The church was consecrated by Cardinal Joseph Höffner in 1973. It can accommodate more than 2,500 people. Their organ which is from the year 1973 was built by the Bonn organ builder Klais. The chiming of the bells of the previous church were taken over.

Neue Synagoge

In der Nacht vom 9. zum 10. November 1938 brannten in Deutschland alle Synagogen, jüdische Geschäfte und Einrichtungen wurden zerstört. Diese grauenhafte „Reichskristallnacht" gab das endgültige Signal zur Judenverfolgung in ganz Deutschland, so auch in Wuppertal. Mehr als ein halbes Jahrhundert mussten die wachsende Zahl jüdischer Einwohner der Stadt warten, bis sie wieder eine eigene Synagoge erhielt. In enger Nachbarschaft der Barmer Gemarker Kirche, der Kirche des „Barmer Bekenntnisses" von 1934, entstand das schlichte Gebäude nach den Plänen des Architekten Christoph Goedeking. Zur Einweihung am 8. Dezember 2002 begrüßte Leonid Goldberg, Vorsitzender der Jüdischen Kultusgemeinde Wuppertal, den deutschen Bundespräsidenten Johannes Rau, den israelischen Staatspräsidenten Mosche Katzaw und Paul Spiegel, den Vorsitzenden des Zentralrats der Juden.

New Synagogue

All synagogues were burned, Jewish shops and facilities were destroyed in Germany in the night of 9th to 10th November 1938. This gruesome "Crystal Night" gave the final signal for the persecution of Jews throughout Germany, in Wuppertal, too. The growing number of Jewish residents of the city had to wait for more than half a century until they obtained their own synagogue once more. The simple building was built in close proximity to the Barmen Gemarker Church, the church of the "Barmen Declaration" of 1934, according to plans by the architect Christoph Goedeking. Leonid Goldberg, chairman of the Jewish Community Wuppertal, welcomed the German Federal President Johannes Rau, the Israeli President Moshe Katzaw and Paul Spiegel, the chairman of the Central Council of Jews, at the inauguration on December 8, 2002.

Städtisches Gymnasium Sedanstraße

1903 konnte das Reform-Realgymnasium der Stadt Barmen sein neues Gebäude am Sedansberg beziehen. Noch heute sind die Schmuckelemente seiner Fassade erhalten. Sie weisen mit ihren Renaissancestilmotiven auf die Entstehungszeit des Gebäudes hin. Mitte des 19. Jahrhunderts wurden in Deutschland die Realgymnasien mit ihren Schwerpunkten Neue Sprachen und Naturwissenschaften gegründet. Sie sollten neben den traditionellen humanistischen Gymnasien die Jugend auf ihre Berufe in Handel und Industrie vorbereiten. Heute besuchen 700 Schülerinnen und Schüler die traditionsreiche Barmer Schule.

Sedan Street Municipal Grammar School

The Reform Real Grammar School of the City of Barmen was able to move into its new building on Sedansberg in 1903. The decorative elements of its facade are preserved even today. They indicate the date of construction of the building through their Renaissancemotifs. Real grammar schools with their focus on new languages and natural sciences were founded in Germany in the middle of the 19th century. They should prepare young people for their jobs in commerce and industry in addition to the traditional humanistic grammar schools. 700 pupils attend the tradition-steeped Barmen School today.

Haus der Jugend mit dem Live Club Barmen

In der Nacht vom 30. zum 31. Mai 1943 zerstörte der verheerende alliierte Bombenangriff auf Barmen die „Ruhmeshalle", die wegen ihrer hohen Kuppel auch „Kleiner Reichstag" genannt wurde. Dabei ging der Bestand der Stadtbibliothek und die Sammlung des Barmer Kunstvereins bis auf wenige Ausnahmen verloren. Das machtvoll wirkende Gebäude war zu Ehren Kaiser Wilhelm I. von 1897-1900 im Stil der Neorenaissance errichtet worden. Beim Wiederaufbau ohne Kuppel in den 1960er Jahren wurde ihr mächtiger Säuleneingang erhalten.

Im Inneren befinden sich großzügige Ausstellungsräume, die bis 2019 u.a. für Ausstellungen des Kunst- und Museumsvereins und des Von der Heydt-Museums genutzt wurden, die Räume der Stadtbibliothek Barmen, des Jugendzentrums und der Veranstaltungssaal des Live Club Barmen, der sich mit kulturellen Veranstaltungen jeglicher Art (im Bild Comedian und Kabarettist Öczan Coşar) einen exzellenten Ruf bis weit über die Stadtgrenzen hinaus erworben hat.

Youth House and Barmen Live Club

The devastating Allied bombing of Barmen on the night of 1943, May 30 to May 31, destroyed the "Hall of Fame" which is also known as the "Little Reichstag" because of its high dome. The stock of the city library and the collection of the Barmer Association was lost with a few exceptions. The powerful looking building was built in honour of Emperor Wilhelm I from 1897-1900 in the neo-renaissance style. Its mighty pillared entrance was preserved during reconstruction without a dome in the 1960s.

There are spacious exhibition rooms which were used for exhibitions of the Art and Museum Association and the Von der Heydt Museum, among others, until 2019, in addition there are the rooms of the Barmen Municipal Library, the youth centre and the event hall of the Barmen Live Club. It has gained an excellent reputation which extends far beyond the city's boundaries through its diverse cultural events (in the picture comedian and cabaret artist Öczan Coşar).

Barmen-Live Bühne vor Rathaus und Barmer „Lichterzauber"

Vor der schönen neoklassizistischen Fassade des Barmer Rathauses finden die zentralen Konzerte und Bühnenereignisse während der Barmer Festwochen Barmen-Live statt. Dann verwandelt sich vor allem in den warmen Sommernächten der große Rathausplatz zum „Barmer Wohnzimmer" und Lebens- und Feierfreude lassen die Zeit vergessen.

Im November taucht eine Installation die Einkaufsmeile „Werth" und den Platz vor dem Barmer Rathaus in eine von Lichterzauber erfüllte Welt. Die Immobilien-Standort-Gemeinschaft ISG Barmen-Werth hat 2017 mit Fördermitteln des Landes NRW eine neue Illumination errichten können. An Garnknäuel erinnern die über 200 verschieden großen Kugeln aus LED-Lichtdrähten, die mit mehr als 16 000 LED-Lichtern einen farbigen Traumhimmel über Straße und Platz schweben lassen. Der traditionelle Weihnachtsmarkt auf dem Rathausplatz sorgt für die entsprechende vorweihnachtliche Stimmung.

Barmen Live Stage in front of the Town Hall and Barmen "Magic Lights"

The central concerts and stage events take place in front of the beautiful neoclassical façade of Barmen town hall during the Barmen festival Barmen Live. The large town hall square then turns into the "Barmen living room", especially on the warm summer nights, and the joy of life and celebration leaves time forgotten.

An installation enchants the shopping mile Werth and the square in front of Barmen town hall in a world filled with magic in November. The real estate location community ISG Barmen-Werth was able to build a new illumination in 2017 with funding from the state of NRW. More than 200 differently sized balls made from LED light wires remind one of balls of wool, which with more than 16,000 LED lights let a colourful dream sky float over the street and square. The traditional Christmas market on the town hall square ensures the appropriate pre-Christmas atmosphere.

Barmer
WeihnachtsMarkt

Hofeshaus Lütterkus-Heidt

Vermutlich gegen Ende des 16. Jahrhunderts ließ der Bleicher und Garnmeister Johann Peter Lütterkus-Heidt dieses älteste erhaltene Fachwerkhaus der Stadt errichten. Die Renaissance-Fachwerkkonstruktion, die Ladeluken mit Kran, der hohe Gewölbekeller mit Brunnen und die Küche mit einer über zwei Geschosse ragenden Herdstelle zeigen den Lebensstil der damals reichsten Familien in Barmen. Das Haus in Privatbesitz wurde mustergültig restauriert und 1986 mit einem Stadtteilfest eingeweiht.

Lütterkus-Heidt Manor House

The bleacher and yarn master Johann Peter Lütterkus-Heidt had this oldest preserved half-timbered house in the city built, presumably towards the end of the 16th century. The Renaissance half-timbered construction, the loading hatches with crane, the high vaulted cellar with well and the kitchen with a hearth over two storeys show the lifestyle of the richest family in Barmen at the time. The privately owned house was restored in exemplary fashion and inaugurated in 1986 with a district festival.

Dicke-Ibach-Treppe zum Ringeltal

Wie der Aufgang zu einer mächtigen Burganlage wirkt die zweiläufige Treppe aus den Barmer Anlagen, dem Ringeltal, zur Joseph-Haydn-Straße. Die Barmer Fabrikanten Friedrich Wilhelm Dicke und Peter Adolph Rudolph Ibach, beide Vorstandsmitglieder des Barmer Verschönerungsvereins, stifteten sie im Jahr 1897. Die imposante Monumentalität entspricht dem Stil repräsentativer Gründerzeitbauten. Sie wird gekrönt von dem hübschen Aussichtspavillon. Das Bronzerelief auf dem Treppenabsatz mit der Darstellung „Christus heilt ein misshandeltes Tier" wurde 2006 gestohlen. Der Barmer Beigeordnete Ludwig Ringel (1808-1881), nach dem das Tal genannt ist, hatte dem Barmer Verschönerungsverein die Ländereien gestiftet.

Dicke-Ibach Flight of Stairs to Ringel Valley

The double flight of stairs from the Barmen grounds, the Ringel valley, to Joseph Haydn Street looks like the ascent to a mighty castle complex. The Barmen factory owners Friedrich Wilhelm Dicke and Peter Adolph Rudolph Ibach, both board members of the Barmen Beautification Association, donated them in 1897. The imposing monumentality corresponds to the style of the representative late nineteenth century buildings. It is crowned by the pretty viewing pavilion. The bronze relief on the landing with the depiction "Christ heals a maltreated animal" was stolen in 2006. The Barmen Lieutenant Ludwig Ringel (1808-1881), after whom the valley is named, had donated the lands to the Barmen Beautification Association.

Barmer Stadtpanorama

In vielen Kurven führt die Obere Lichtenplatzer Straße von der Innenstadt Barmens zum Toelleturm-Viertel und nach Lichtscheid auf die Südhöhen der Stadt. Der Blick vom Aussichtspunkt Barmen zeigt deutlich die topographische Lage der Stadt im langgestreckten Tal der Wupper, von dem aus sich die Bebauung eng und steil zu den Höhen erstreckt: die Nordhöhen der Stadt mit dem Nordpark, den Wassertürmen vom Hatzfeld und in der Mitte den Fahrradweg Nordbahntrasse über die Viadukte der stillgelegten früheren Bahnstrecke Düsseldorf-Derendorf–Dortmund Süd, lokal bekannt als Wuppertaler Nordbahn.

Barmen City Panorama

Obere Lichtenplatzer Straße leads in many curves from the city centre of Barmen to the Toelle Tower district and to Lichtscheid on the southern heights of the city. The view from the Barmen viewpoint clearly shows the topographical position of the city in the elongated valley of the Wupper from which the building development extends narrowly and steeply to the heights: the northern heights of the city with North Park, the water towers of Hatzfeld and in the middle the Northern railway line cycle way over the viaducts of the disused former railway line Düsseldorf-Derendorf-Dortmund South, locally known as the Wuppertal northern railway.

Toelleturm

1864 gründeten wohlhabende Barmer Bürger den Barmer Verschönerungsverein, der bis heute für die Barmer Anlagen verantwortlich ist. Auf dem Plateau in der Nähe des Bergbahnhofs der früheren Barmer Bergbahn ließen die Kinder des Textilfabrikanten Ludwig-Ernst Toelle (1823-1886) den nach ihm benannten Aussichtsturm errichten. Er ist 26,5 Meter hoch, die Treppe zur Aussichtsplattform hat 146 Stufen. Wegen Baufälligkeit war der Turm seit den späten 1970er Jahren lange geschlossen, sollte gar abgerissen werden. Aber der Barmer Verschönerungsverein konnte ihn restaurieren lassen und seit 1990 ist er meist an Wochenenden geöffnet.

Toelle Tower

Wealthy Barmen citizens founded the Barmen Beautification Association, which is still responsible for the Barmen facilities, in 1864. The children of the textile manufacturer Ludwig-Ernst Toelle (1823-1886) had the lookout tower, which is named after him, built on the plateau near the hill station of the former Barmen hill railway. It is 26.5 metres high, the stairs to the observation deck have 146 steps. The tower had been closed since the late 1970s due to disrepair, it should even have been demolished. But the Barmen Beautification Association was able to have it restored and since 1990 it has usually been open at the weekends.

Vorwerk-Park

Der Barmer Unternehmer Adolf Vorwerk (1808-1881) ließ bei seiner Villa im Toelleturmviertel 1881 einen weitläufigen Park anlegen. Zu ihm gehören ein früherer Steinbruch mit Steilkante zum Murmelbachtal, ein Teich und eine Grotte. 1895 kam am Rand der Barmer Anlagen ein Laubengang hinzu. Von der Parkhöhe aus öffnet sich ein romantischer Blick über die Wälder des Tals. Seit 1907 pflanzte man Rhododendren und Azaleen verschiedenster Arten an. 2001 wurde der Park der Öffentlichkeit übergeben, weil die Familie Vorwerk ihn in eine Stiftung einbrachte. Zur Rhododendronblüte im Frühjahr entfaltet sich eine märchenhafte Farbenpracht.

Vorwerk Park

Barmen entrepreneur Adolf Vorwerk (1808-1881) had a spacious park created at his villa in the Toelle Tower district in 1881. A former quarry with a steep cliff to the Murmelbach valley, a pond and a grotto belong to it. A pergola was added on the edge of the Barmen grounds in 1895. A romantic view opens up over the forests of the valley from the height of the park. Various species of rhododendrons and azaleas have been planted since 1907. The park was opened to the public in 2001 because the Vorwerk family converted it into a foundation. A magical blaze of colour unfolds in spring as the rhododendron bloom.

Unterbarmer Friedhof Mausoleum Carl Toelle

Der Unterbarmer Friedhof war seit seiner Eröffnung 1822 bevorzugter Begräbnisort Barmer Bürger. Die wohlhabenden Familien unter ihnen besaßen eine Prachtallee mit besonders auffallenden Grabmälern. Erhalten ist noch das Mausoleum, das der Düsseldorfer Bildhauer Josef Hammerschmidt (1873-1926) mit der tragischen Figur des Hagen von Tronje und dem trauernden Sänger Volker aus der Nibelungensage als Totenwächter errichtete. Carl Toelle war der zweite Sohn Hugo Toelles, zu dessen Erinnerung der Barmer Toelleturm errichtet wurde.

Unterbarmen Cemetery Mausoleum Carl Toelle

The Unterbarmen cemetery has been the preferred burial place of the citizens of Barmen since its opening in 1822. The wealthy families among them had a magnificent avenue with particularly striking tombs. The mausoleum, erected by the Düsseldorf sculptor Josef Hammerschmidt (1873-1926), with the tragic figure of Hagen of Tronje and the mourning singer Volker from the Nibelungen Saga as a guard for the dead is still preserved. Carl Toelle was the second son of Hugo Toelle in whose memory the Barmen Toelle Tower was built.

Unterbarmer Hauptkirche

1822 vereinigten sich in Unterbarmen Lutheraner und Reformierte Evangelische Gemeindemitglieder aus ihren Elberfelder Gemeinden zu einer der ersten neuen „unierten" Vereinigt-Evangelischen Kirchengemeinden im Rheinland. Sie folgten damit einer Anregung des preußischen Königs Friedrich Wilhelm III. von 1817, um die oft kämpferisch betonten Glaubensunterschiede zu überwinden. Durch die neue Gemeindegründung konnten sich die Unterbarmer den weiten Weg zu den Elberfelder Kirchen sparen; auch hatten sie gute Erfahrungen in der gemeinsamen Armenpflege während des Hungerjahres 1816 gemacht. 1832 öffnete die neue große „Hauptkirche", nach Entwürfen von Architekt Heinrich Hübsch in dem damals modernen „Rundbogenstil" errichtet, eines der ersten Beispiele des Historismus. Nach ihrer Zerstörung im 2. Weltkrieg wurde sie wiederaufgebaut, jedoch ohne die spitzen Zeltdächer ihrer beiden Türme.

Unterbarmen Main Church

Lutherans and Reformed Protestant parishioners united in Unterbarmen from their Elberfeld communities to form one of the first new "unified" United Evangelical church congregations in the Rhineland in 1822. They followed a suggestion from 1817 by the Prussian King Friedrich Wilhelm III to overcome the often aggressively emphasized differences of faith. The formation of the church community enabled those from Unterbarmen to save themselves the long way to the Elberfeld churches; they had also had good experiences in joint care of the poor during the famine year 1816. The new large "main church" designed by architect Heinrich Hübsch in the then modern "round arch style" opened in 1832 as one of the first examples of historicism. It was rebuilt after its destruction in World War II but without the pointed tent roofs of its two towers.

Bitte nicht
einsteigen!
03
Völklinger Straße

Schwebebahnstation Völklinger Straße

In der ursprünglichen, vom Jugendstil geprägten Bauweise „formidentisch" rekonstruiert, wurde die Schwebebahnstation Völklinger Straße am 21. Mai 2012 wieder in Betrieb genommen. Von ihr aus sind die nördlichen Unterbarmer Wohnbezirke zu erreichen und in der Talsohle die Friedrich-Engels-Allee mit dem Polizeipräsidium. Vor dem Ersten Weltkrieg hieß die Brücke beim Bahnhof Kaiserbrücke, später wurden sie und die Straße nach der saarländischen Industriestadt benannt.

Völkinger Street Suspension Railway Station

The suspension railway station Völklinger Street, reconstructed in the original art nouveau style of "form identical" construction, was put back into service on 21 May 2012. The northern Unterbarmen residential districts can be reached from there as well as the Friedrich-Engels-Allee with the police headquarters at the valley bottom. The bridge was called the Kaiserbrücke station before the First World War, it was later named after the Saarland industrial city together with the street.

Treppe an der Buchenstraße

93 Stufen hoch führt die Treppe an der Buchenstraße hinauf in die Wohnsiedlung an der Hardt und am Loh. Sie wurde 1910 gebaut und gehört zum alten Unterbarmer Färberviertel, in dem viele Färbereien und Garnveredelungsbetriebe ihren Standort hatten. Hier weitet sich das enge Wuppertal zum Haspeler Bogen. Auf seinen Wiesen wurden noch im 19. Jahrhundert Garne gebleicht.

Flight of Stairs on Buchen Street

The 93 steps of the flight of stairs on Buchen Street lead up to the housing estate on the Hardt and at Loh. It was built in 1910 and belongs to the old Unterbarmen Färber district where many dyeing and yarn refining companies were located. The narrow Wuppertal widens to the Haspeler curve here. Yarns were bleached in its meadows in the 19th century.

Junior Uni mit Skulptur „Stück für Stück" von Tony Cragg

Auf dem Brachgelände eines früheren Textilunternehmens an der Wupper in Unterbarmen konnte 2013 das einladende, schöne Gebäude der 2008 gegründeten Wuppertaler Junior Uni eingeweiht werden. Das Architektenteam um Christoph Godeking und Johannes Niedworok schuf diesen farbenprächtigen, oval geschnittenen Raumkörper direkt am Wupperufer neben der Schwebebahnstation Loh mit einem Foyer und 16 Seminar- und Fachräumen, in denen Kinder und Jugendliche von vier bis zwanzig Jahren das Forschen vor allem in naturwissenschaftlichen Fächern lernen können. Das allein durch private Mittel finanzierte Bildungsinstitut bietet ganzjährig an die 4000 Kurse an. Dozenten, Professoren, aber auch Studenten unterrichten hier. Zum zehnjährigen Geburtstag der Junioruni schenkte der in Wuppertal lebende, weltbekannte Bildhauer Tony Cragg die Skulptur „Stück für Stück", die mit ihrer leuchtend roten Farbe ein Blickfang auf dem Platz vor der Junior Uni ist. Sie kann als Sinnbild für die Unermüdlichkeit menschlichen Lernens von Anfang an und Stück für Stück gelten.

Junior Uni with the Sculpture "Little by Little" by Tony Cragg

The inviting, beautiful building of the Wuppertal Junior University, founded in 2008, was inaugurated in 2013 on the fallow site of a former textile company on the Wupper in Unterbarmen. The team of architects led by Christoph Godeking and Johannes Niedworok created this colourful, oval shaped space directly on the banks of the Wupper next to the Loh suspension railway station with a foyer and 16 seminar and specialist rooms where children and adolescents from four to twenty years of age can learn how to research, especially in natural science subjects. The educational institution, financed solely by private funds, offers around 4,000 courses throughout the year. Lecturers, professors, but also students teach here. The world famous sculptor Tony Cragg, who lives in Wuppertal, donated the sculpture "Stück für Stück" ("Little by Little") to commemorate the tenth anniversary of Junioruni. With its bright red colour it is an eyecatcher on the square in front of the Junior University. It can be considered a symbol of the tirelessness of human learning little by little from the start.

Skulpturenpark Waldfrieden mit Villa Herberts

Die skulpturale Form der Villa Waldfrieden hat wohl den Ausschlag gegeben, dass Tony Cragg, international bekannter Bildhauer und von 2009 bis 2013 Rektor der Kunstakademie Düsseldorf, Haus und Gelände der Villa Waldfrieden für das Projekt eines Skulpturenparks entdeckte. Im mit hohen Laubbäumen bestandenen Hang richtete er einen dem Publikum geöffneten Park für seine eigenen monumentalen Skulpturen und die anderer zeitgenössischer Bildhauer ein. Über dem Platz des früheren Schwimmbads ließ Tony Cragg durch den Architekten Rudolf Hoppe ein hohes kubusartiges Gebäude aus Stahlträgern und Glaswänden als Ausstellungshalle und Konzertraum entwerfen. Im ehemaligen Gärtnerhaus des Parks richtete er das Café Podest ein. Seit September 2008 ist der Park geöffnet, im Waldgelände entstanden zwei weitere Pavillons. Die Villa Waldfrieden wurde durch den Unterbarmer Lackfabrikanten Dr. Kurt Herberts (1901-1989) nach dem Zweiten Weltkrieg in fließenden Formen errichtet, die anthroposophischem Bauwillen nahestehen. Ihr Architekt war Werkkunstschullehrer Franz Krause (1897-1979), der gemeinsam mit Oskar Schlemmer und Willi Baumeister während nationalsozialistischer Zeit - trotz Berufsverbot als Künstler - in der Lackfabrik in Sicherheit arbeiten konnte.

Waldfrieden Sculpture Park with Herberts Villa

The sculptural form of the Waldfrieden Villa was probably the reason that Tony Cragg, internationally known sculptor and from 2009 to 2013 Headmaster of the Academy of Arts in Düsseldorf, discovered the house and grounds of the villa for a sculpture park project. He set up a park, which is open to the public, on the slope with high deciduous trees for his own monumental sculptures and those of other contemporary sculptors. Tony Cragg had a tall, cube-like building of steel girders and glass walls designed by the architect Rudolf Hoppe as an exhibition hall and concert hall above the site of the former swimming pool. He set up the Café Podest in the former gardener's house. The park has been open since September 2008 and two more pavilions have sprung up in the forest. Paint manufacturer Dr. med. Kurt Herberts (1901-1989) had the Waldfrieden Villa built after the Second World War in flowing forms that are close to the anthroposophical building style. The architect was technical art school teacher Franz Krause (1897-1979) who was able to work together with Oskar Schlemmer and Willi Baumeister in safety in the paint factory despite a professional ban as an artist during the National Socialist era.

Alte Kornmühle in Unterbarmen

Die Kornmühle in Unterbarmen wurde 1682 errichtet. Das große Gebäudeensemble steht unter Denkmalschutz und war in den letzten Jahrzehnten Domizil eines beliebten Restaurants. Der Stadtteil Unterbarmen war im 19. Jahrhundert Zentrum der Färbereien, die vor allem das berühmte „Türkisch-Rot" färbten. Die Schwebebahn fährt auch heute noch dicht an den hohen Fenstern der alten Fabrikanlagen vorbei.

Old Grain Mill in Unterbarmen

The grain mill in Unterbarmen was built in 1682. The large building complex is under a protection order and has been the home of a popular restaurant in recent decades. The suburb of Unterbarmen was the centre of the dye works which mainly dyed the famous "Turkish red" in the 19th century. The suspension railway passes close to the tall windows of the old factories even today.

Sachsenröder-Werk

Die Gebäude der Firma Sachsenröder befinden sich wie viele andere Fabrikanlagen des 19. Jahrhunderts direkt am Wupperufer, häufig begrenzen Gebäudemauern auch den Fluss direkt. Gustav-Heinrich Sachsenröder gründete die Firma 1881, die heute in vierter Generation geführt wird. Im Anfang produzierte Sachsenröder Spezial-Pergamentpapiere, um 1900 stellte der Gründer als erster in der Welt Endlos-Vulkanfiber her. Vulkanfieber, wegen seiner Elastizität und Härte auch als „Lederstein" bezeichnet, hat als Grundstoff Zellstoff oder Baumwolle und ist ein Trägermaterial von Schleifscheiben.

Sachsenröder Plant

The buildings of the Sachsenröder company are directly on the banks of the Wupper like many other factories of the 19th century, building walls often border directly onto the river as well. Gustav-Heinrich Sachsenröder founded the company in 1881 which is now run by the fourth generation. Sachsenröder produced special parchment papers in the beginning, the founder was the first in the world to produce endless vulcanised fibre around 1900. Vulcan fibre which is also known as "leather stone" because of its elasticity and hardness has pulp or cotton as base material and is a carrier material for grinding wheels.

Hohenstein

Der steile Dolomitfelsen am Südrand des Stadtteils Rott entstand vor 380 Millionen Jahren im Erdzeitalter des Devon aus einem gewaltigen Korallenriff. Der Gesteinsgürtel dieses Riffes zieht sich im Norden Wuppertals vom Neandertal bis an die östliche Grenze von Schwelm. Da Kalkstein zur Verhüttung von Eisen nötig ist, wurde er überall im Stadtgebiet abgebaut, was heute allerdings nur noch in Dornap geschieht. Die Initiative des „Fördervereins historische Parkanlagen Wuppertal" ließ 2009 den kleinen zugewucherten Park beim „Hohenstein", der einen wunderschönen, faszinierenden Blick auf Barmen bot, wieder freischneiden, so dass Besucher sich heute wieder hier sonnen und den Ausblick auf Wuppertal genießen können.

Hohenstein

The steep dolomite rocks at the southern edge of the district of Rott originated 380 million years ago from a huge coral reef in the geological era of Devon. The rock belt of this reef runs from the Neandertal to the eastern border of Schwelm north of Wuppertal. Limestone was mined throughout the urban area as it is needed for the smelting of iron which only happens in Dornap today, however. The initiative of the "Historical Wuppertal Parks Society" had the small overgrown park at the "Hohenstein", which offered a beautiful, fascinating view of Barmen, cut free again in 2009 so that visitors can sunbathe here once more today and enjoy the view of Wuppertal.

Museum auf der Hardt

Schon 1799 gründeten reformierte und lutherische Pfarrer in Elberfeld einen Missionsverein; ihm folgte 1818 die Barmer Missionsgesellschaft, die 1825 die Barmer Missionsschule gründete. Mit weiteren Missionsvereinen schlossen sich die Barmer und Elberfelder zur Rheinischen Missionsgesellschaft zusammen, aus der sich in den 1990er Jahren die VEM Vereinte Evangelische Mission bildete. Zu ihr gehören heute selbständige Kirchen aus Afrika, Asien und Deutschland. Das Barmer Missionshaus auf der Hardt sandte Missionare vor allem nach Afrika, Indonesien und Neuguinea. Von ihren Reisen brachten sie Anschauungstücke der ursprünglichen Kulte mit, die heute oft in den Herkunftsländern nicht mehr vorhanden sind. Aus ihnen entstand das „Museum auf der Hardt" mit außerordentlichen Exponaten der Völkerkunde.

Museum on the Hardt

Reform and Lutheran pastors founded a missionary association in Elberfeld as early as 1799. It was followed in 1818 by the Barmen Missionary Society which founded the Barmen Missionary School in 1825. Barmen and Elberfeld came together with other missionary associations to form the Rhenish Missionary Society from which the VEM United Evangelical Mission was formed in the 1990s. Independent churches from Africa, Asia and Germany belong to it today. The Barmen mission house on the Hardt sent missionaries to Africa, Indonesia and New Guinea in particular. From their travels they brought with them visual pieces from the original cults, which are often no longer present in the countries of origin today. The "Museum on the Hardt" with extraordinary exhibits of ethnology resulted from them.

Bismarckturm „Götterdämmerung" auf der Hardt

Der Düsseldorfer Architekt Wilhelm Kreis (1873-1955) nannte seinen Entwurf für einen Bismarckturm „Götterdämmerung". Nach dem Tod des früheren Reichskanzlers Bismarck im Jahr 1898 wurden zur Erinnerung an den legendären Reichsgründer von 1871 in ganz Deutschland und in den deutschen Kolonien Bismarcktürme errichtet. Von den insgesamt 240 Türmen entstanden allein 47 nach dem Entwurf „Götterdämmerung". Diesen wählten auch die Bürger in Barmen und Elberfeld und errichteten 1907 durch Spenden das Gemeinschaftswerk genau auf der Grenze zwischen beiden Städten auf der Hardt. Dort steht er bis heute und verrät viel über den bürgerlichen Nationalstolz in der ausgehenden Kaiserzeit.

Bismarck Tower "Twilight of the Gods" on the Hardt

The Düsseldorf architect Wilhelm Kreis (1873-1955) called his draft for a Bismarck tower "Götterdämmerung" ("Twilight of the Gods"). Bismarck towers were erected throughout Germany and in the German colonies after the death of former chancellor Bismarck in 1898 to commemorate the legendary empire founder of 1871. Of the total of 240 towers, 47 were created according to the design "Twilight of the Gods". The citizens of Barmen and Elberfeld also chose this and erected the joint venture, as a result of donations, on the Hardt right on the border between the two cities in 1907. It is still standing there today and reveals a lot about the bourgeois national pride in the late imperial period.

Hardt während 24h-Live mit Elisenturm und Tropenhaus

Im September öffnen sich Wuppertaler Unternehmen, Stadtviertel und Gebäude dem 24-Stunden-Live-Spektakel zum gemeinsamen Feiern und Kennenlernen der eigenen Stadt. Auch der Elisenturm auf der Hardt im ältesten städtischen Park Wuppertals (seit 1807) überhaupt und die Gewächshäuser des Botanischen Gartens werden zu Event-Orten. Auf den Fundamenten einer abgebrochenen Windmühle ließ der Elberfelder Fabrikant und Stadtrat Engelbert Eller einen Sternwartenturm errichten. Das mit schlanken Pilastern verzierte elegante Gebäude widmete er „Elise", Elisabeth Ludovika von Bayern (1801-1873), der Gemahlin des Preußenkönigs Friedrich Wilhelm IV. Dieser liebte die Romantik. Neben dem Turm entstand 1875 ein „Landhaus" im Stil italienischer Villen. Der Botanische Garten ging aus dem Schulgarten hervor, der 1890 auf der Hardt angelegt wurde. Zum 200jährigen Bestehen des Parks errichtete die Stadt auf dem Gelände der früheren Stadtgärtnerei die neuen Gewächs- und Schauhäuser mit dem Tropenhaus.

Hardt during 24h live with the Elisen Tower and Tropical House

Wuppertal companies, neighbourhoods and buildings open their 24 hour live spectacle in September to celebrate together and get to know their own city. The Elisen Tower on the Hardt in the oldest urban park in Wuppertal (since 1807) and the greenhouses of the botanical garden also become event locations. The Elberfeld manufacturer and city councillor Engelbert Eller had an observatory tower built on the foundations of a broken windmill. The elegant building, decorated with slender pilasters, was dedicated to "Elise", Elisabeth Ludovika of Bavaria (1801-1873), the wife of the Prussian king Friedrich Wilhelm IV. This one loved romance. A "country house" in the style of Italian villas was built next to the tower in 1875. The Botanical Garden emerged from the school garden, which was created on the Hardt in 1890. The city built the new greenhouses and showhouses with the tropical house on the grounds of the former city nursery for the 200th anniversary of the park.

Passionsspiele auf der Hardt

An jedem Karfreitag verwandelt sich die Elberfelder Innenstadt zur Kulisse eines Passionsspiels, das am Platz der Laurentiuskirche beginnt und auf der Hardt endet und zu dem sich viele Zuschauer an den Straßenrändern einfinden. Seit 1980 hat diese Prozession schon Tradition, die Mitglieder der Missione Cattolica Italiana, der Italienischen Katholischen Gemeinde in Wuppertal, ins Leben gerufen haben. Viele Familien der italienischen Zuwanderer seit den 1960er Jahren haben ihre Wurzeln auf Sizilien und in Süditalien, wo die Karfreitagsprozessionen üblich sind. Laien spielen die Hauptrolle, alle paar Jahre wird für die Darstellung des Jesus von Nazareth eine neue Besetzung gesucht.

Passion Plays on the Hardt

Elberfeld's city centre becomes the setting for a passion play that begins at the Laurentius church square and ends on the Hardt every Good Friday with many spectators lining the streets. This procession has traditionally been initiated by members of the Missione Cattolica Italiana, the Italian Catholic Community in Wuppertal, since 1980. Many families of Italian immigrants since the 1960s have their roots in Sicily and Southern Italy where Good Friday processions are common. Lay people play the main role, a new casting for the depiction of Jesus of Nazareth is carried out every few years.

Justizbehörden
Schauspielhaus
Elberfeld-Zentrum

Legobrücke über die Schwesternstraße und Nordbahntrasse am Engelnberg

Als sei sie aus monumentalen Legosteinen erbaut, so perfekt räumlich illusioniert hat 2011 der Wuppertaler Streetart-Künstler Martin Heuwold die Unterseite einer Betonbalkenbrücke über der Schwesternstraße in Elberfeld bemalt. Geboren 1976 in Wuppertal, ausgebildet als Maler und Lackierer wurde er mit seinen Graffiti-Bildern international bekannt. Die „Legobrücke" erhielt 2012 den Förderpreis des Deutschen Fassadenpreises. Die Brücke gehörte zur 1991 stillgelegten Strecke der Rheinischen Bahn im Norden Wuppertals, die seit 2006 von dem Verein Wuppertalbewegung zur 23 Kilometer langen sogenannten Nordbahndtrasse umgebaut wurde.

Durch eine tiefe Schlucht und einen 197 Meter langen Tunnel beim Engelnberg führt der Fahrradweg auf der stillgelegten Nordbahnstrecke, die seit 1879 als Rheinische Strecke im Norden der Stadt dicht an Häusern vorbei und hoch über Viadukte von Düsseldorf über Wuppertal-Vohwinkel nach Dortmund-Hörde führte. Sie wurde im Jahr 1991 für den Güterverkehr, 1999 auch für den Personenverkehr stillgelegt. Dem hartnäckigen Einsatz der 2006 gegründeten „Wuppertalbewegung" ist es zu verdanken, dass die 23 Kilometer lange Strecke mit großartigen Blicken auf die Stadt im Tal heute als Fahrradweg genutzt wird und auch weiter in Zukunft bis nach Langerfeld geführt wird. Sie hat Anschluss an das nordrheinwestfälische Fahrradnetz.

Lego Bridge over Schwestern Street and Northern Rail Line at Engelnberg

Wuppertal street artist Martin Heuwold painted the underside of a concrete beam bridge over Schwestern Street in Elberfeld in 2011 as if it were made of monumental Lego bricks, such perfect spatial illusion. Born in 1976 in Wuppertal, trained as a painter and varnisher, he became internationally known through his graffiti paintings. The "Lego Bridge" received the 2012 Promotion Prize of the German Facade Award. The bridge belonged to the 1991 decommissioned route of the Rhenish Railway in north Wuppertal that the Wuppertal Movement Association has been rebuilding into the 23 kilometre long so-called cycle street "Nordbahntrasse" since 2006.

The cycle path on the disused Northern Rail Line, which as the Rhenish route in the north of the city has gone close to houses and high over viaducts from Düsseldorf via Wuppertal-Vohwinkel to Dortmund-Hörde since 1879, goes through a deep gorge and a 197 metre long tunnel at Engelnberg. It was decommissioned in 1991 for freight, in 1999 also for passenger transport. It is thanks to the persistent efforts of the "Wuppertal Movement", founded in 2006, that the 23 kilometre long route with great views of the city in the valley is now used as a cycle path and will continue to Langerfeld in the future. It is connected to the North Rhine-Westphalian bicycle network.

MOMENT
MIT UTOPIA AN 81190
MIT 3 EURO*.

Nordbahntrasse am Mirker Bahnhof und Tanztunnel

An den seit den 1990er Jahren verfallenden Bahnhöfen entstand durch die Eröffnung der Nordbahntrasse im Jahr 2014 neues, vielfach einfallsreiches Leben. Im ehemaligen Bahnhof Mirke zog die Initiative „Utopiastadt" ein, die im Ziegelfachwerkbau aus dem Jahr 1882 eine Anlaufstelle für „kreative Stadtentwicklung" eröffnete. Hier finden Projekte und Unternehmungen freier Gruppen Räume für Ideen und Visionen. Kultur- und Musikereignisse machen den alten Bahnhof zu einem bekannten Treffpunkt. In ehrenamtlicher Arbeit wurde das Gebäude renoviert; im Erdgeschoss zog das „Café Hutmacher" ein. Im Sommer ist das Freigelände auf den früheren Gleisanlagen bei Spaziergängern, Fahrradfahrern und vielen Menschen aus der Nachbarschaft sehr beliebt.

Im nur 500 Meter entfernten Tunnel Dörrenberg kann gelegentlich auch bei farbigen Lichtilluminationen und Musik getanzt werden.

Northern Rail Line at Mirker Station and the Dance Tunnel

New and often resourceful life was created at the railway stations which had been decaying since the 1990s due to the opening of the Northern Rail Line in 2014. The "Utopia City" initiative moved into the former Mirke station which opened a focal point for "creative urban development" in the timber frame construction from 1882. Projects and ventures of free groups find spaces for ideas and visions here. Cultural and musical events make the old train station a well-known meeting place. The building was renovated through volunteer work, Café Hutmacher moved in on the ground floor. The outdoor area on the former tracks is very popular with walkers, cyclists and many people in the neighbourhood in summer.

One can occasionally also dance with colourful lighting and music in the Dörrenberg Tunnel, which is just 500 metres away.

Schwebebahnstation Landgericht mit Gerichtsgebäude

Der Bahnhof „Landgericht" ist eine der drei Haltestellen, die bei der generellen Rekonstruktion der Schwebebahn Ende der 1990er Jahre wieder ganz „formidentisch" ihr altes Aussehen erhalten haben und unter Denkmalschutz stehen. Die Bahnhöfe stammten alle aus der Jahrhundertwende und verbanden technische Sachlichkeit mit dem grafischen Linienspiel von Wänden und Tragelementen. So passt der Bahnhof bis heute gut zu dem ehrwürdigen, 47 Meter langen Arkadengang des Landgerichtsgebäudes, das bewusst 1844 auf der Grenze zwischen den Schwesterstädten auf einer Wupperinsel errichtet wurde, allerdings Barmen näher als Elberfeld. Im Stile der italienischen Frührenaissance errichtete es der Schinkelschüler Carl Ferdinand Busse (1802-1868), der Direktor der Berliner Bauakademie. Bis heute ist die Gerichtsinsel Standort von Landgericht und Amtsgericht Wuppertal.

Suspension Railway Station District Court with Court Buildings

The station "District Court" is one of the three stops that was given its old appearance back again, "completely identical in form", in the general reconstruction of the suspension railway at the end of the 1990s and is under a protection order. The stations were all from the turn of the century and combined technical objectivity with the graphically linear walls and supporting elements. The station, thus, fits well to the venerable 47 meter long arcade passage of the district court building which was deliberately built on the border between the sister cities on a Wupper island, closer to Barmen than Elberfeld however. The Schinkel student Carl Ferdinand Busse (1802-1868), the director of the Berlin Building Academy, built it in the style of the early Italian Renaissance. The judicial island is still the location of the provincial and the district court of Wuppertal.

Schwebebahnstation Kluse

Beim Bombenangriff auf Elberfeld am 25. Juni 1943 wurde die Schwebebahnstation Kluse zerstört. Erst mit der Neukonstruktion des Schwebebahngerüsts wurde auch in der „Kluse" 1999 wieder ein Bahnhof gebaut. Der Düsseldorfer Architekt und Hochschullehrer Bernward von Chamier entwarf seine kühne Konstruktion in der Kluser Kurve neben Schauspielhaus und Cinemaxx-Kinopalast. Die Träger des Bahnhofs enden in mächtigen Betonsockeln in Form unregelmäßiger Pyramiden, in denen die Bahnhofstechnik aufgenommen ist. Mit seinen hellen Glaswänden ist „Kluse" ein schlüssiges, auch spannungsvolles Beispiel moderner Technik-Architektur.

Suspension Railway Station Kluse

The suspension station Kluse was destroyed in the bomb attack on Elberfeld on 25 June 1943. A railway station was first built again in the "Kluse" in 1999 with the new construction of the suspension railway framework. The Düsseldorf architect and university professor Bernward von Chamier designed his bold construction in the Kluser Curve next to the theatre and the Cinemaxx cinema palace. The bearers of the station end in mighty concrete bases in the form of irregular pyramids in which the station technology is incorporated. "Kluse" is a coherent and also exciting example of modern architecture with its bright glass walls.

Oberbarmen
20
VON BAUM
VON BAUM

Schwebebahn an der Bembergbrücke

Wie in eine dunkle Schlucht fährt die Schwebebahn zwischen Bembergbrücke und Bahnhof Döppersberg an den hohen Fabrik- und Kontorhäusern der Hofaue vorbei. Die Hofaue war die frühere Viehweide der mittelalterlichen Hofburg Elberfeld. Im 18. Jahrhundert bauten sich wohlhabende Elberfelder hier im Osten der Stadt schöne Villen im Bergischen Barockstil. Als Elberfeld sich Mitte des 19. Jahrhunderts an die Eisenbahnstrecke von Düsseldorf nach Dortmund anschloss, nutzten Fabriken und Lagerhäuser den kurzen Weg zum Bahnhof über die Bembergbrücke. Die „Hofaue" wurde für alle Textilhändler der Welt erste Adresse, denn hier entstand ein Zentrum der Textilherstellung, vor allem von Konfektionsware, wie die der Firma von Baum. Früher erblickte man beim Schwebebahnfahren hinter den Fenstern die vielen Näherinnen. Seit Ende der 1960er Jahre setzte das Sterben der Wuppertaler Textilindustrie ein. Die Häuserschlucht der Hofaue fand vielfach andere Nutzer, Firmen, Studios aber auch die Bergische Musikschule der Stadt.

Suspension Railway at Bemburg Bridge

The suspension railway between Bemberg Bridge and Döppersberg Station passes the high factory and office buildings of the Hofaue as if in a dark ravine. The Hofaue was the former cattle pasture of the medieval Elberfeld Hofburg. In the 18th century wealthy people in Elberfeld built beautiful villas in the Bergisch Baroque style in the east of the city. Factories and warehouses made use of the short route to the station via the Bemberg Bridge when Elberfeld joined the railway line from Düsseldorf to Dortmund in the mid-19th century. The "Hofaue" became the first choice for all the textile merchants in the world because a centre of the textile production had developed here, above all ready-to-wear such as that of the company von Baum. One used to see the many seamstresses behind the windows as one rode on the suspension railway. The death of the Wuppertal textile industry began in the late 1960s. The house canyon of the Hofaue found many other users, companies, studios but also the Bergisch Music School of the city.

AGGRESSIV
AUSLÖSER
BERUHIGUNG
FREUDE
VERBOT
ZUR WEHR SETZEN
ZORN
BEGEISTERUNG
BRUDER
NÄHE
VERGEBE
SCHLECHTES GEWISSEN
BESCHÜTZEN
JAUCHZEN
EHRE
FA
ERSCHRECKEN
UNSCHULD
HEIMAT
LIEBKOSEN

„Scala" Holsteiner Treppe

Nahezu 500 Treppen und Treppenwege gehören zum Wuppertaler Stadtgebiet. Wie die Holsteiner Treppe mit ihren 112 Stufen verbindet sie für Fußgänger gradlinig und schnell die Straßen an steilen Berghängen. Die Holsteiner Treppe wurde in der ganzen Welt berühmt, weil der Aktionskünstler Horst Gläsker ihren Stufen verschiedene Farben gab. Sie wechseln kunstvoll wie in einer Skala zwischen hellen und dunklen, warmen und kühlen Farben und tragen jeweils einen Begriff für Emotionen, Gefühle und komplexe Stimmungen. Beim Heraufsteigen regen sie so die Menschen an, über sich und die Welt nachzudenken. Über die „Scala" gelangt man zur Flensburger Straße und weiter bis zum Platz der Republik auf der Höhe des Ostersbaums.

"Scala" Holsteiner Steps

Almost 500 flights of stairs and stepped paths belong to the Wuppertal city area. Just like the Holsteiner steps with its 112 steps which connects the streets on steep mountain slopes for pedestrians, straight-lined and fast. The Holsteiner flight of stairs became famous all over the world because the action artist Horst Gläsker gave different colours its steps. They change artistically as if in a scale between light and dark, warm and cool colours and each carry a term for emotions, feelings and complex moods. As they ascend they encourage people to think about themselves and the world. One reaches Flensburger Street via the "Scala" and further on to the Platz der Republik at the elevation of Ostersbaum.

Gerechtigkeitsbrunnen von Bernhard Hoetger auf dem Platz der Republik

Als Exerzierplatz richteten die Elberfelder auf dem damals noch unbebauten Plateau des Engelnbergs einen freien großen Platz ein, der auch für Volksfeste genutzt wurde. 1899 wurde er als Park ausgebaut, und der Elberfelder Bankier und Kunstsammler August von der Heydt (1851-1929) stiftete zum Fest des 300-jährigen Bestehens der Stadt den großen „Gerechtigkeitsbrunnen". Auf ihm ließ er die Bronzefigur „Adorantin" (Verehrende) von Bernhard Hoetger (1874-1949) aufstellen. Sie ist etwa 4 Meter hoch und überragt feierlich das auf drei eisernen Löwen ruhende Brunnenbecken. Während des 2. Weltkriegs wurde die Figur eingeschmolzen. Großzügige Spendenmittel ermöglichten 2011 eine Rekonstruktion nach Abbildungen. Diese wurde 2012 wieder aufgestellt. Bernhard Hoetger war mit August von der Heydt befreundet. Er erhielt durch seine Vermittlung zahlreiche Aufträge für Elberfelder Bürger und machte den Sammler mit dem Werk der 1907 verstorbenen Malerin Paula Modersohn-Becker bekannt. Von ihr kamen später mehr als 20 Bilder aus seiner Sammlung ins Von der Heydt-Museum.

Justice Fountain by Bernhard Hoetger in the Platz of the Republik

TThe people of Elberfeld set up a parade ground on the free large square on the plateau of the Engelnberg which was still undeveloped then and was also used for public festivals. It was expanded as a park in 1899 and the Elberfeld banker and art collector August von der Heydt (1851-1929) donated the great "justice fountain" to the celebration of the 300th anniversary of the city. He had the bronze figure "Adorantin" (worshipful) by Bernhard Hoetger (1874-1949) set up on it. It is about 4 metres high and towers ceremonially over the fountain basin resting on three iron lions. The figure was melted down during World War II. Generous donations enabled a reconstruction according to illustrations in 2011. This was set up again in 2012. Bernhard Hoetger was a friend of August von der Heydt. He received numerous commissions for Elberfeld citizens through his mediation and introduced the collectors to the work of the painter Paula Modersohn-Becker who died in 1907. More than 20 of her pictures from his collection came in the museum Von der Heydt later on.

ERGO

Elberfelder Rathaus, heutiges Verwaltungshaus Elberfeld und Jubiläumsbrunnen am Neumarkt

Am 24. Oktober 1900 kam Kaiser Wilhelm II. für zweieinhalb Stunden ins Tal, um am Bahnhof Oberbarmen den Start der Schwebebahn zu feiern und anschließend die Barmer Ruhmeshalle sowie das neue Elberfelder Rathaus einzuweihen. Das alte Rathaus am Turmhof, in dem seit 1902 das Von der Heydt-Museum sein Domizil hat, war zu klein geworden. Die Professoren Heinrich Reinhardt und Georg Süßenguth von der Technischen Universität Berlin hatten die Pläne für das im historisierenden Stil mit Elementen der Spätgotik und Renaissance errichtete Gebäude gemacht. Der Marktverkauf auf dem Neumarkt findet außer sonntags täglich statt. Bis 1802 befand sich hier der Elberfelder Friedhof.

1895 feierte der Elberfelder Verschönerungsverein sein 25-jährige Bestehen. Einer seiner Mitbegründer, der kunstbegeisterte Bankier August von der Heydt, hatte mit seiner Ehefrau Selma auf einer Reise nach Trient den dortigen Neptunbrunnen auf dem Domplatz gesehen und initiierte eine Spendenaktion, um auf dem Neumarkt eine Nachbildung dieses Brunnens aufzustellen. Der Bildhauer Leo Müsch (1846-1911) gestaltete den Entwurf für den 11,5 Meter hohen Brunnen aus rotem Mainsandstein mit der krönenden Figur des Meeresgottes. Seine barocke, unverblümte Darstellung der männlichen Anatomie führte zu heftigen Protesten des Bürgertums und der Kirche. Von der Heydt ließ deshalb Akanthusblätter über den angeblich schamverletzenden Zonen anbringen. Diese wurden jedoch später wieder entfernt. 2014 wurde der Brunnen mit all seinem mythischen Meerespersonal wieder restauriert. Seit 2000 steht er unter Denkmalschutz.

Elberfeld Town Hall, Current Administration Building in Elberfeld and Jubilee Fountain at New Market

Emperor Wilhelm II came to the valley for two and a half hours to celebrate the start of the suspension railway at the Upper Barmen station and then inaugurate the Barmen Hall of Fame and the new Elberfeld Town Hall on October 24, 1900. The old town hall at the Turmhof where the Von der Heydt Museum has been located since 1902 had become too small. The professors Heinrich Reinhardt and Georg Süßenguth from the Technical University of Berlin had made the plans for the building built in the historical style with elements of late Gothic and Renaissance. The market sale at the New Market takes place every day except Sundays. The Elberfeld cemetery was located here until 1802.

The Elberfeld Beautification Society celebrated its 25th anniversary in 1895. One of the co-founders, the art-loving banker August von der Heydt, and his wife Selma had seen the Neptune fountain on the cathedral square on a trip to Trient and initiated a fundraiser to erect a replica of this fountain at New Market. The sculptor Leo Müsch (1846-1911) designed the 11.50 metre high fountain made of red Main sandstone with the crowning figure of the Sea God. His baroque, blunt portrayal of male anatomy led to violent protests from the bourgeoisie and the church. Von der Heydt therefore had acanthus leaves applied over the allegedly shame infringing zones. These were removed later, however. The fountain was restored with all its mythical marine personnel in 2014. It has been under a preservation order since 2000.

Begegnungsstätte Alte Synagoge

Im Laufe des 19. Jahrhunderts wuchs mit der Industriestadt auch der Anteil der jüdischen Bevölkerung. In Elberfeld konnte sie 1865 ihre schöne Synagoge an der Genügsamkeitsstraße errichten. In der sogenannten „Reichskristallnacht" vom 8./9. November 1938 wurde sie vom nationalsozialistischen Mob vollkommen zerstört. Ein Modell der Synagoge ist heute in der Begegnungsstätte Alte Synagoge ausgestellt. Auf den Mauerresten errichteten 1994 die Kölner Architekten Peter Busmann und Godfried Haberer ein neues, eindrucksvolles Gebäude-Ensemble. Die Begegnungsstätte „Alte Synagoge" hat den Auftrag, an die Geschichte, Kultur und Religion der Juden in Wuppertal und im Bergischen Land zu erinnern. Seit 2011 vermittelt die Dauerausstellung „Thora und Textilien" mit vielen Dokumenten und Objekten einen Eindruck vom jüdischen Leben in der Stadt. Dem Trägerverein der Begegnungsstätte gehören mehr als 20 Institutionen an, darunter Kirchen und die Jüdische Kultusgemeinde Wuppertal. Sie forscht zum Alltag des Judentums und zum Schicksal der früher hier Lebenden. Sie bietet viele Veranstaltungen zur Weiterbildung und für Schulprojekte und macht namhafte Veröffentlichungen.

Old Synagogue Meeting Place

As the industrial city grew in the course of the 19th century so did the proportion of the Jewish population. They were able to build their beautiful synagogue on Frugality Street in Elberfeld in 1865. It was completely destroyed by the National Socialist mob in the so-called "Crystal Night" from 8th/9th November 1938. A model of the synagogue is on display in the meeting place Old Synagogue, today. The Cologne architects Peter Busmann and Godfried Haberer erected a new, impressive ensemble of buildings on the remains of the walls in 1994. The meeting place "Old Synagogue" has the mission to serve as a reminder of the history, culture and religion of the Jews in Wuppertal and in Bergisch Land. The permanent exhibition "Torah and Textiles" with its many documents and objects has provided an impression of Jewish life of the city since 2011. The host association of the meeting place is comprised of more than 20 institutions, including churches and the Jewish Community of Wuppertal. It researches the everyday life of Judaism and the fate of those who used to live here. It offers many events for further education and school projects and makes well-known publications.

Rathausgalerie und Bronzelöwe von Christoph Daniel Rauch

Feuer speien mit Hilfe eines Gasrohrs konnten die beiden Löwen aus Eisenguss, die seit 1833 auf der Freitreppe des Früheren Elberfelder Rathauses, dem heutigen Von der Heydt-Museum, standen. Sie waren nach einem Modell des berühmten klassizistischen Bildhauers Christian Daniel Rauch (1877-1857) gegossen worden. 1877 als verkehrsbehindernd entfernt, hatten sie wechselnde Verlegenheitsstandorte in der Stadt. Bei den Transporten wurde der eine von ihnen zerstört, 1948 rettete den übriggebliebenen Günther Muthmann von einem Schrottplatz und stellte ihn vor seiner Firma C. Blumhardt auf. Dort konnte er bis 1993 bleiben. Eine großartige Spendenaktion des Bergischen Geschichtsvereins und der Westdeutschen Zeitung machte seine Restaurierung möglich. Seit 1994 steht er als „Stadtlöwe" auf dem Willy-Brandt-Platz an der Rückseite des Elberfelder Rathauses. An der Nordseite des Platzes eröffnete 1994 die Rathaus-Galerie als erstes großes Einkaufszentrum Elberfelds.

Town Hall Gallery and Bronze Lion by Christoph Daniel Rauch

The two cast iron lions which stood on the external steps of the former Elberfeld Town Hall since 1833, today's Von der Heydt Museum, could spit fire with the help of a gas pipe. They were cast according to a model by the famous classicist sculptor Christian Daniel Rauch (1877-1857). Removed in 1877 as a hindrance, they have had changing, awkward locations in the city. One of them was destroyed during transport, Günther Muthmann saved the remaining one from a junkyard in 1948 and set it up in front of his company C. Blumhardt. It was able to stay there until 1993. A splendid donation campaign by the Bergisch Historical Association and the West German Newspaper made its restoration possible. It has been standing as a "city lion" in Willy Brandt Platz at the back of the Elberfeld town hall since 1994. The Town Hall Gallery opened in 1994 on the north side of the square as the first large shopping centre in Elberfeld.

Zuckerfritz-Denkmal von Ulle Hees auf dem Kerstenplatz

An einer Ecke des Kersten-Platzes in der Nähe des Neumarkts sitzt das frühere Original der Zuckerfritz auf seiner Schubkarre, als müsse er sich ausruhen. Die Wuppertaler Bildhauerin Ulle Hees (1941-2012) schuf die Bronzefigur, die an den Elberfelder Fritz Pohl (1831-1906) erinnert . Wie die „Mina Knallenfalls", auch von Ulle Hees, gehörte der Dienstmann - immer mit derselben Taffetkappe - zum Zentrum der wachsenden Großstadt. Er war als Botengänger und Zusteller tätig und nahm immer gern Zuckerstücke - ein solches hält er im Denkmal in der Hand - und auch Zigarrenstummel an. Er starb 1906 an einer Lungenentzündung im Städtischen Krankenhaus Elberfeld.

Sugar Fritz Memorial by Ulle Hees at Kerstenplatz

The former original, the Sugar Fritz, who sits on his wheelbarrow as if he had to rest is at one corner of Kersten Square near New Market. The Wuppertal sculptor Ulle Hees (1941-2012) created the bronze figure reminiscent of Elberfeld Fritz Pohl (1831-1906). The servant - always with the same taft cap - belonged to the centre of the growing city just like "Mina Knallfalls" which is also by Ulle Hees. He worked as a messenger and deliverer and always liked to accept pieces of sugar - one of which he holds in his hand in the memorial - and cigar stubs as well. He died of pneumonia in Elberfeld Municipal Hospital in 1906.

Mina Knallenfalls-Denkmal von Ulle Hees

Sie schaut ein wenig spöttisch, auch selbstbewusst die Fußgänger auf der Alten Freiheit an, wenn sie vom Hauptbahnhof oder der Schwebestation Döppersberg in die City eilen. Mancher kann der Versuchung nicht widerstehen, ihr auf die Schulter zu klopfen. Anders als die Bronzefigur des „Zuckerfritzes" von Ulle Hees am Kersten-Platz hat Mina Knallenfalls nicht wirklich existiert. Aber der Elberfelder Mundartdichter und Lithograph Otto Hausmann (1837-1916) machte die Weberin Mina zur Heldin einer Elberfelder Geschichte. Vielleicht ist aber auch seine Großmutter Vorbild gewesen. Ulle Hees, die noch weitere Figuren im Wuppertaler Stadtbild geschaffen hat, hat sich in die Welt der Frauen in dem häufig überschwemmten Armenviertel „An der Fuhr" am Wupperufer, im 19. Jahrhundert eingefühlt.

Mina Knallenfalls Monument by Ulle Hees

She looks a little mockingly as well as confident at the pedestrians on Alten Freiheit when they hurry from the main station or suspension railway station Döppersberg into the city. Some people cannot resist the temptation to pat her shoulders. Mina did not really exist unlike the bronze figure of "Zuckerfritz" by Ulle Hees at Kersten Platz. But the Elberfeld dialect poet and lithographer Otto Hausmann (1837-1916) made the weaver Mina the heroine of an Elberfeld story. Maybe his grandmother was also a role model. Ulle Hees, who has created even more figures in the Wuppertal cityscape, had introduced himself to the 19th century world of women on the Fuhr, the often flooded slums on the banks of the Wupper.

CITY-ARKADEN
RESERVED
KLAUSER
H&M
akzenta
Alte Freiheit
Bergische Musikschule
Benedict
HUSSEL

Alte Freiheit mit Cityarkaden

Die höchste Besucherfrequenz Wuppertaler Innenstädte misst man an der Alten Freiheit. Hier wurden 2001 in einem großen Neubauprojekt die City-Arkaden eröffnet, in der wie auf einem großen Markplatz in mehreren Etagen Einzelhandelsgeschäfte und Gastronomie einen attraktiven Branchenmix bieten. Die 1965 gegründete ECE-Projektmanagement GmbH &Co. KG der Otto-Gruppe betreibt das Center, das mit seinem sich nach oben weitenden Kubus stadtbildprägend ist.

Alte Freiheit with City Arcade

The highest visitor frequency of Wuppertal's inner cities is measured at the Alte Freiheit. The city arcade in which retail stores and restaurants offer an attractive mix of stores on several floors just as in a large marketplace was opened here in a major new building project in 2001. ECE-Projektmanagement GmbH & Co. KG of the Otto Group, founded in 1965, operates the centre which shapes the cityscape with its upward extending cube.

City-Plaza am neu gestalteten Döppersberg

2018 wurde das vollkommen neu gestaltete Areal des Bahnhofsvorplatzes zwischen Wupperbrücke am Döppersberg und Hauptbahnhof der Öffentlichkeit übergeben. Nicht alle nahmen die radikale Neugestaltung mit dem durchbrochenen Mauerwerk an den Verbindungswegen, Galerien und Treppen und der mächtigen, sich wie eine Schale oder Blüte nach oben öffnenden Skulptur des Kaufhaus- und Bürogebäudes mit Zustimmung auf. Das international tätige Architekturbüro Chapman Taylor, das in der ganzen Welt Städtebauprojekte und Einkaufszentren plant, hat dem platzbestimmenden Gebäude in Elberfeld eine Außenfassade aus Messing-Verbund-Platten gegeben. Diese sind wie die gestanzten Lochkarten früherer Jacquard-Bandwebstühle übersät mit kleinen Öffnungen, die der Fassade eine in sich unruhige Struktur geben. So greift die avantgardistische Architektur ein altes Element der Textilherstellung im Tal auf. Gegenüber der Treppe und den klassizistischen Fassaden der Gebäude der früheren Elberfelder Bahnhofsdirektion und des Wuppertal-Instituts sowie dem Hauptbahnhofsgebäude entsteht ein spannungsvoller Gegensatz zu den gebogenen Wänden der Kaufhausschale.

City Plaza at the Newly Designed Döppersberg

The completely redesigned area of the station forecourt between the Wupper Bridge at Döppersberg and the main railway station was handed over to the public in 2018. The radical redesign of the open plan masonry along the connecting lanes, galleries and staircases and the mighty sculpture of the department store and office building opening up like a shell or blossom was not met with approval by everyone. Chapman Taylor, an international architecture firm that plans urban development projects and shopping centres around the world, gave the plaza defining building in Elberfeld an exterior façade made of brass composite panels. These are covered with small openings like the punched hole cards of earlier jacquard looms that give the facade a rather restless structure. The avant garde architecture thus takes up an old element of textile production in the valley. An exciting contrast to the curved walls of the department store shell emerged opposite the flight of stairs and the classical façades of the buildings of the former Elberfeld RailwayStation Management and the Wuppertal Institute as well as the main station building.

Busbahnhof am Hauptbahnhof

Wie Bündel von Mikado-Stäben tragen weiße Säulen die Platte des neuen Busbahnhofs am Döppersberg. Über ihn führen Lichtkuppeln Tageslicht in die darunter liegende Bahnhofsvorhalle. Die Säulenbündel selbst tragen die langen ovalen Dächer der Bus-Haltestellen. Von der Galerie der Platte hat man einen interessanten Blick auf die „City Plaza" mit dem avantgardistischen Kaufhausgebäude. Es wird bewusst, dass der Elberfelder Bahnhof auf einer Stufe am Steilhang des 146 Meter hohen Döppersbergs über der Talsohle liegt. Züge aus Düsseldorf kamen bis 1838 nur bis zum Bahnhof Steinbeck. Die Verbindung zum Hauptbahnhof wurde erst durch einen schluchtartigen Durchstich 1848 geschaffen.

Bus Station at the Main Railway Station

Bundles of jack straw like white columns carry the platform of the new bus station in Döppersberg. Overhead light domes lead daylight into the station concourse below. The column bundles themselves carry the long oval roofs of the bus stops. One has an interesting view of the "City Plaza" with the avant garde department store building from the gallery of the platform. It becomes clear that Elberfeld station is located on a level place on the steep slope above the valley floor of 146 metre high Döppersberg. Trains from Düsseldorf only came up to the Steinbeck station until 1838. The connection to the main station was first created by a gorge like cut in 1848.

Historische Stadthalle auf dem Johannisberg

Der Elberfelder Stadtbaurat Wilhelm Mäurer, Leiter des Elberfelder Bauwesens von 1870 bis 1900 entwarf im Stil der italienischen Spätrenaissance das gerne auch als „Stadtschloss Elberfeld" bezeichnete prachtvolle Gebäude. Es ist ein Höhepunkt historisierender Architektur in Europa und besitzt einen der schönsten Konzertsäle mit außerordentlich guter Akustik. Nach dem 2. Weltkrieg wurden ihre reichen Innendekorationen weiß übertüncht. Aber unter Leitung des Wuppertaler Architektenpaars Will und Chris Baltzer konnte sie ab 1992 mit großem Aufwand und äußerst sorgfältig restauriert werden. 1995 wurde sie der Öffentlichkeit wieder übergeben, ein „grandioser Schwanengesang" der Gründerzeitpoche. In festliche Hochstimmung versetzen die schimmernd polierten schwarzen Granitsäulen mit ihren flachen Kompositkapitellen die mit Blüten, Masken und Voluten goldfarben geschmückt sind. Zwischen ihnen wölben sich baldachinartig die flachen Kuppen der Decken. Hier lässt es sich seit mehr als 100 Jahren im besten Sinne wandeln! Selbst die historischen, mächtigen Lampenschalen mit ihren hängenden Blütenkelchen wurden restauriert und bewundernswert ist die Deckenmalerei.

Historical City Hall on Johannisberg

The Elberfeld City Head of Municipal Planning Wilhelm Mäurer, director of the Elberfeld building industry from 1870 to 1900, designed the magnificent building often called the "Elberfeld City Palace" in the style of the Italian late Renaissance. It is a highlight of historical architecture in Europe and has one of the most beautiful concert halls with exceptionally good acoustics. The rich interior decorations were whitewashed after the Second World War. They were restored from 1992 on with great effort and meticulous care under the direction of the Wuppertal architects Will and Chris Baltzer. It was returned to the public in 1995, a "grand swan song" of the years of rapid industrial expansion in Germany in the 19th century The shimmering polished black granite columns with their flat composite capitals, decorated in gold with flowers, masks and volutes, add a festive atmosphere. The flat domes of the ceilings arch like a canopy between them. Changes have been made here, in the best sense, for more than 100 years. Even the historic, powerful lampshells with their hanging calyx have been restored; the ceiling painting is also admirable.

Ball Tango-Argentino in der Historischen Stadthalle

Ende der 1990er Jahre zog das Tango-Fieber im Tal ein. Ein Zentrum dieses leidenschaftlichen Tanzes bildete sich im Café Ada am Ölberg im Norden der Stadt. Aber das Tango-Festival wird seit 1998 in der Historischen Stadthalle gefeiert und internationale Stars des kunstvollen, faszinierenden Tanzes kommen dann in die Stadt.

Tango Argentino Ball in the Historical City Hall

Tango fever came to the valley at the end of the 1990s. A centre of this passionate dance was formed in Café Ada on the Ölberg in the north of the city. But the Tango Festival has been held in the Historic City Hall since 1998 and international stars of the artful, fascinating dance come to the city.

Vollmann
Group
BHC - FANS
OPDAHÜH
FANCLUB BERGISCHE HANDBALL LÖWEN
NICHTRAUCHER
STORCH
DKB
WILKINSON
SWORD
LIQUI MOLY
HANDBALL-BUNDESLIGA
Stauder

Unihalle mit Handball Bundesligaspiel zwischen dem BHC 06 und THW Kiel

15 Jahre nach der Gründung der Bergischen Universität wurde die „Unihalle" als Mehrzweckhalle 1987 eröffnet. Ursprünglich als Trainingshalle zur Ausbildung der Studierenden geplant, gehört sie heute zu den großen Sport und Veranstaltungshallen. Bis zu 4 097 Besuchern bietet sie Platz. Vom Rockfestival, Messen bis zum Hallenfußball bietet sie Raum für viele Großereignisse. Das alljährliche Schülerrockfestival und die festlichen traditionellen Erstsemester-Begrüßungen finden hier ebenso statt wie Spiele der Handball-Bundesliga. Der Bergische Handball-Club 06, ein gemeinschaftlicher Profi-Handballverein der bergischen Städte Wuppertal und Solingen, wurde 2006 durch eine Teilfusion durch Übertritt des Managements, des Kaders und des Hauptsponsors des LTV Wuppertal zum Solinger Rivalen SG Solingen gegründet. Die Heimspiele des BHC 06 werden in der Wuppertaler Unihalle, sowie der Solinger Klingenhalle ausgetragen.

Unihalle with Handball Bundesliga Match between BHC 06 and THW Kiel

The "Unihalle" was opened as a multi-purpose hall in 1987 fifteen years after the founding of the Bergisch University. Originally planned as a training hall for the education of students it is one of the largest sports and event halls today. It has space for up to 4,097 visitors. It offers space for many major events from rock festivals to trade fairs and indoor football. The annual school students rock festival and traditional first semester festive greetings take place here as well as national league handball matches. The Bergisch Handball Club 06, a joint professional handball club from the Bergisch cities of Wuppertal and Solingen, was founded in 2006 through a partial merger due to the transfer of management, the squad and the main sponsor of LTV Wuppertal to Solingen rival SG Solingen. The home games of the BHC 06 are held in the Wuppertal Unihalle as well as the Solingen Klingenhalle.

Die Bergische Universität

Im burgartig angelegten Gebäudeensemble mit ihrem hohen Bibliotheksturm wurde 1974 auf dem Grifflenberg im Süden Elberfelds die Gesamthochschule eröffnet. Fachhochschulen der Region, wie die Pädagogische Hochschule, die Ingenieurschulen und die Werkkunstschule wurden Fachbereiche der Bergischen Universität, wie sie seit 2003 heißt. Sie wurde von dem NRW-Ministerpräsidenten Johannes Rau gegründet, der sie schon als Oberbürgermeister von Wuppertal angeregt hat. Viele interdisziplinäre Fächer und Studiengänge sind in ihrem Studienangebot, außerdem die klassischen Universitätsfächer außer Medizin und Jura. Fast 22 000 Studierende besuchen die Universität, an der mehr als 400 Professoren lehren. Die Terrassen des Mensagebäudes bieten einen fantastischen Blick über Elberfeld. Auf den Höhen des Grifflenberges befinden sich weitere Insitutsräume in den ehemaligen Kasernen der Bundeswehr und am Haspel direkt am Wupperufer.

The Bergisch University

The Bergisch University was opened as a comprehensive university in the castle- like building ensemble with its high library tower in 1975 on the Grifflenberg in the south of Elberfeld. Universities of applied sciences in the region such as the College of Education, the engineering schools and the Applied Art School became departments of the Bergisch University, as it has been called since 2003. It was founded by Johannes Rau, the NRW Prime Minister, who had already encouraged it as Lord Mayor of Wuppertal. Many interdisciplinary subjects and degree courses are included in the courses of study as well as the classical university subjects apart from medicine and law. Almost 22,000 students attend the university where more than 400 professors teach. The terraces of the refectory building offer a fantastic view over Elberfeld. There are further institute rooms in the former army barracks on the slopes of the Grifflenberg and on the Haspel directly on the bank of the Wupper.

Kommunikationszentrum „die börse" in Unterbarmen im denkmalgeschützten Fabrikgebäude

Überregional bekannt ist „die börse", eines der ältesten soziokulturellen Zentren der Region. Dieses Forum der freien Kulturarbeit entstand zuerst im früheren, denkmalgeschützten Verwaltungsgebäude des Schlachthofs Elberfeld. Dort war es oft erheblichen Anfeindungen ausgesetzt. 1996 konnte „die börse" ein altes, ebenfalls unter Denkmalschutz stehendes Fabrikgebäude an der Straße „Wolkenburg" beziehen, wo es heute mit einer Fülle von Angeboten und Veranstaltungen für alle Generationen der Stadt und weit über die Region hinaus bekannt ist. Das Gebäude, eine Fabrikhalle mit Shed-Dach, wurde 1910 im Art Déco-Stil errichtet und hat zur Straße hin eine burgartige Bruchsteinfassade, deren Giebel über den Fenstern gedrückte Spitzbogenform haben. Der Name der Straße „Wolkenburg" bezieht sich auf den steilen Felsen eines Bergsporns, der zwischen Unterbarmen und Kluse über dem Tal aufragt. Auf ihm legte ein Elberfelder Kaufmann einen Privatpark an, den der Förderverein Historische Parkanlagen Wuppertal e.V. wieder zugänglich machte.

"die börse" Communication Centre in Unterbarmen in a Listed Factory Building

One of the oldest socio-cultural centres in the region, "the börse", is known nationally. This forum for free cultural work was first created in the former, administrative building of the Elberfeld slaughterhouse which is listed. It was often exposed to considerable hostility there. "die börse" moved into an old factory building on "Wolkenburg" street in 1996 which is also a listed building and where it is known far beyond the region today for a wealth of offers and events for all generations of the city. The building, a factory hall with a saw tooth roof, was built in Art Deco style in 1910 and has a castle- like stone façade facing the street whose gables have a depressed pointed arch shape above the windows. The name of the road "Wolkenburg" (cloud castle) refers to the steep rock of a mountain spur which rises between Unterbarmen and Kluse above the valley. A businessman from Elbe created a private park on it which was made accessible by the Wuppertal Historical Park Areas Association.

Moderne Architektur: Barmenia Verwaltungsgebäude

Ihre Ursprünge hat die Barmenia Versicherungsgruppe in der 1904 gegründeten Gewerbekrankenkasse zu Leipzig. 1931 fusionierte diese mit verschiedenen Lebens- und Krankenversicherern, unter ihnen die Barmer Krankenkasse, zum Leipziger Verein-Barmenia Krankenversicherung für Beamte, freie Berufe und Mittelstand. Nach dem Zweiten Weltkrieg wurde 1958 die Barmenia Allgemeine Versicherungs- AG gegründet. 1971 kam der Sitz der Barmenia Lebensversicherung A.G. von Hamburg nach Wuppertal. Ab 2004 erfolgten Erweiterung und Neubau auf dem Barmenia-Gelände bei laufendem Betrieb. Die drei markanten Gebäuderiegel sind stadtbildprägend. Im parkartigen Gelände über den Lüftungsanlagen stehen sich wie zwei Stücke aus gewellten monumentalen Schläuchen die Skulpturen des weltberühmten Wuppertaler Bildhauers Tony Cragg gegenüber.

Modern Architecture: Barmenia Administration Building

The Barmenia Insurance Group has its origins in the Trade Health Insurance in Leipzig which was founded in 1904. This merged together with various life and health insurers - among them the Barmer Health Insurance - in 1931 to establish the Leipzig Association-Barmenia Health Insurance for civil servants, freelancers and the middle class. Barmenia General Insurance AG was founded after the Second World War in 1958. The headquarters of Barmenia Life Insurance AG came from Hamburg to Wuppertal in 1971. Expansion and new construction took place on the Barmenia site from 2004 during ongoing operations. The three striking construction blocks are define the cityscape. The monumental sculptures by the world famous sculptor Tony Cragg are in the park in front of them like two pieces of corrugated monumental ventilation tubes.

Schwebebahnstation Ohligsmühle und Büro und Geschäftsbauten

Futuristisch wirkt die avantgardistische Architektur der Schwebebahnstation Ohligsmühle. Thyssen Engineering entwickelte seine Konstruktion nach dem Entwurf des Wuppertaler Architekturbüros Rathke im Jahr 1974. Ihr gegenüber auf dem Südufer der Wupper entstanden neben dem alten IHK-Gebäude aus den 1920er Jahren 2017 die neuen Bank- und Geschäftsgebäude, die das Stadtbild entscheidend veränderten.

Suspended Railway Station Ohligsmühle and Commercial Buildings

The avant-garde architecture of the Ohligsmühle suspension railway station appears futuristic. Thyssen Engineering developed its construction in 1974 according to the design of the architectural office Rathke Wuppertal. The new banking and commercial buildings that significantly changed the cityscape emerged across the Wupper on the south bank in 2017 next to the old IHK building built in the 1920s.

Von der Heydt-Museum

Von 1828 bis 1842 dauerte der Bau des ersten repräsentativen Rathauses in Elberfeld. Der Architekt Johann Peter Cremer (1785-1863), ein bedeutender Vertreter des rheinischen Klassizismus, errichtete das Gebäude nach dem Vorbild Florentiner Paläste. Bis 1902 nutzten die Elberfelder das Gebäude als Rathaus, danach zog der 1892 gegründete Museumsverein ein. Von Anfang an galt ein besonderes Augenmerk dem Ankauf zeitgenössischer Kunst. So kamen schon früh Werke der Expressionisten des "Blauen Reiter" und der „Brücke" ins Haus. Aus dem „Städtischen Museum Elberfeld" wurde 1929 nach dem Zusammenschluss von Barmen und Elberfeld zu Wuppertal das Städtische Museum Wuppertal. 1946 schloss sich der 1866 gegründete Barmer Kunstverein mit dem Elberfelder Museumsverein zusammen. Nach mehrjährigem Um- und Erweiterungsbau durch die Architekten Peter Busmann und Godfried Haberer, auch Architekten der Barmer Neuen Synagoge, öffnete das Museum 1991 wieder und stellte auf den Treppensockeln die beiden Figuren von Tony Cragg auf. Sie zeigen Formen in Verwandlung und bilden einen reizvollen Kontrast zu dem Löwengeländer aus Gusseisen und dem Rhythmus der Rundbogen-Fassade. Die Collage „Blaue Flasche" im Treppenhaus (Seite 104) gestaltete Tony Cragg bereits 1982 aus Plastikfundstücken der Rheinufer. Das Wuppertaler Museum hat seinen Namen nach der Elberfelder Bankiersfamilie von der Heydt, die ihm bedeutende Kunstwerke gestiftet hat. Es gehört heute zu den führenden Museen des Rheinlands.

The Von der Heydt Museum

The construction of the first representative town hall in Elberfeld took from 1828 to 1842. The architect Johann Peter Cremer (1785-1863), an important representative of Rhenish classicism, built the building based on the model of Florentine palaces. The inhabitants of Elberfeld used the building as the town hall until 1902 after which the Museum Society, founded in 1892, moved in. Special attention was paid to the purchase of contemporary art from the beginning. Thus, early works of the expressionists, the "Blue Rider" and the "Bridge", came into the building. The "Municipal Museum Elberfeld" became the Municipal Museum Wuppertal in 1929 after the merger of Barmen and Elberfeld. The Barmen Art Association, founded in 1866, merged with the Elberfeld Museum Association in 1946. The museum reopened in 1991 after several years of reconstruction and extension by the architects Peter Busmann and Godfried Haberer, architects of the Barmen New Synagogue, who placed the two figures by Tony Cragg at the bottom of the stairs. They show forms in transformation and form a delightful contrast to the lion railing of cast iron and the rhythm of the arched facade. The collage "Blue Bottle" in the stairwell (page 104) was designed by Tony Cragg in 1982 from pieces of plastic found on the banks of the Rhine. The Wuppertal Museum takes its name from the Elberfeld banking family von der Heydt who donated important works of art to it. It is one of the leading museums in the Rhineland today.

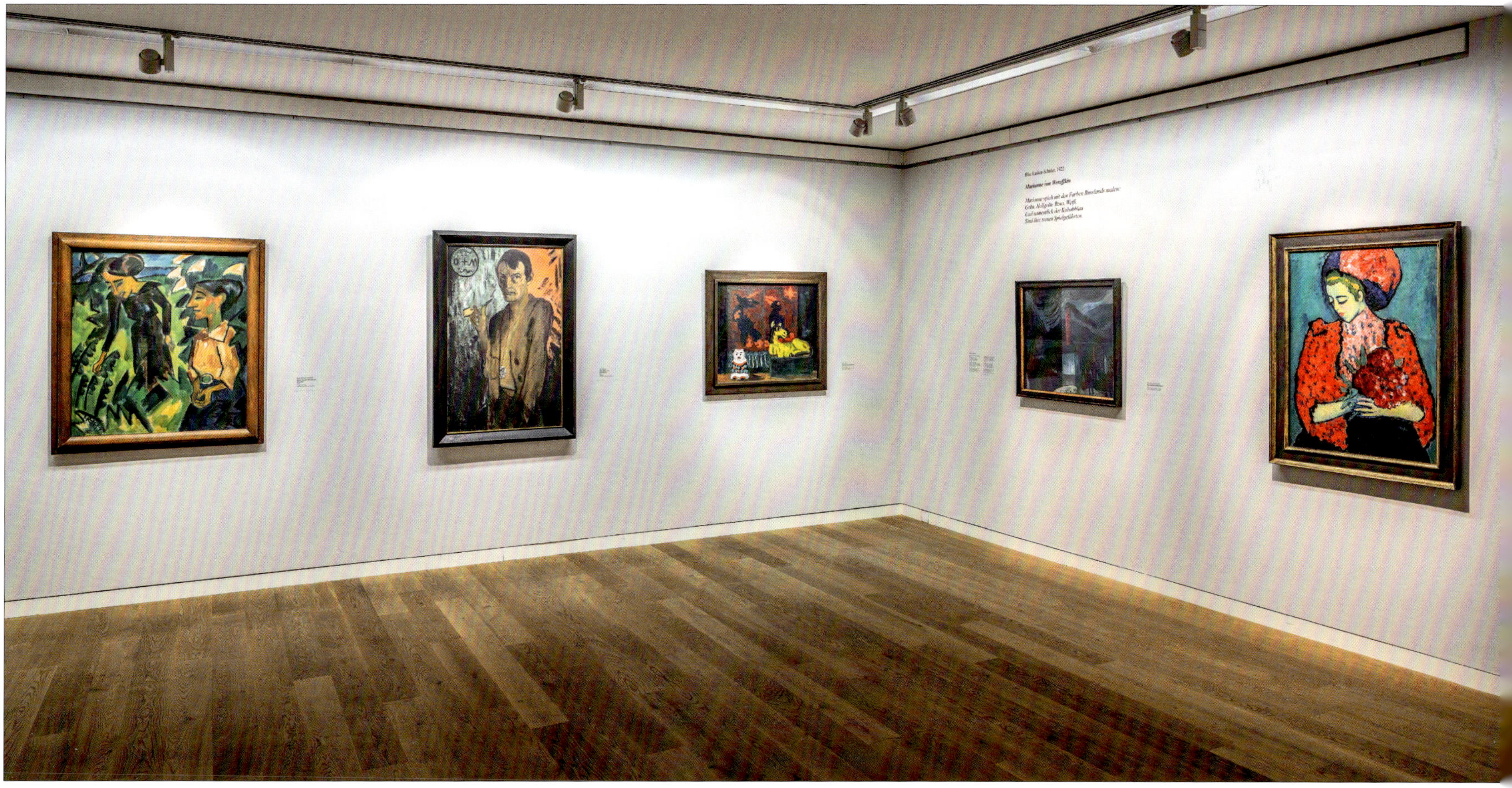

Jankel Adlers Porträt von Else Lasker-Schüler im Von der Heydt-Museum

Der junge, aus Polen stammende Künstler Jankel Adler (1895-1949) besuchte die Barmer Kunstgewerbeschule, bevor er in Düsseldorf studierte und ein berühmter Künstler der Avantgarde wurde. In Berlin lernte er die aus Elberfeld stammende Expressionistin Else Lasker-Schüler (1869-1945) kennen, für die er das Porträt malte. Transparent wirkende kubistische verbinden sich mit illusionierten Collageelementen. Die Lyrikerin schrieb dafür über Adler ein Gedicht. Der Barmer Kunstverein erwarb das Bild 1926 für seine Sammlung. Die Nationalsozialisten beschlagnahmten es 1937 mit 1 500 anderen Bildern aus der Wuppertaler Sammlung, die teilweise in den europäischen Galeriehandel kamen. 1986 konnte das Bild aus einer Pariser Privatsammlung zurückerworben werden. 2019 feierte die Stadt Wuppertal das Gedenken an die Dichterin zu ihrem 150jährigen Geburtstag mit zahlreichen Veranstaltungen und einer umfassenden Ausstellung ihres dichterischen und malerischen Werks im Von der Heydt-Museum.

Jankel Adler's Portrait of Else Lasker-Schüler in the Von der Heydt Museum

The young Polish artist Jankel Adler (1895-1949) attended the Barmen School of Applied Arts before studying in Düsseldorf and becoming a famous avant-garde artist. He met the Elberfeld born Expressionist Else Lasker-Schüler (1869-1945) in Berlin for whom he painted the portrait. Transparent cubist elements are combined with illusionistic collage elements. The poet wrote a poem about Adler. The Barmen Art Association acquired the painting in 1926 for its collection. The Nazis seized it in 1937 together with 1,500 other pictures from the 'Wuppertal Collection', some of which entered the European gallery trade. The picture was bought back from a Parisian private collection in 1986. The city of Wuppertal celebrated the memory of the poet on her 150th birthday in 2019 with numerous events and a comprehensive exhibition of her poetic and pictorial work in the Von der Heydt Museum.

Skulptur „Ein neuer erfolgreicher Tag" auf dem „Schwarzer Fleck" genannten Platz vor dem Sasse Haus

Keine Ruhe findet der Handstand des energischen, sportlichen und jung wirkenden Geschäftsmanns am Kasino-Kreisel in der Nähe von Banken und Finanzamt. Denn die Krawatte der farblich gefassten Bronzefigur wurde immer wieder gestohlen, auch der schwarze Aktenkoffer, den er neben sich gestellt hat. Der belgische Bildhauer und Konzeptkünstler Guillaume Bijl, 1946 in Antwerpen geboren, war von 2001 bis 2011 Professor an der Kunstakademie Münster. Seine humoristische Figur wurde 2007 von der Sparda Bank West der Stadt Wuppertal gestiftet, die sie mitten im Getriebe auf einem 1,4 Meter hohen schwarzen Sockel aufstellte. „Schwarzer Fleck" heißt der Platz, weil er hier nach Neuausrichtung der Kreuzung einen dunklen Asphaltbelag erhalten hat. „Krawattenmann" wird die Skulptur genannt, aber ihr vom Künstler gewählter Name „Ein neuer erfolgreicher Tag" weist auf ihre symbolische Bedeutung hin.

Sculpture "A New Successful Day" on the square called "Schwarzer Fleck" in front of the Sasse Building

The handstand of the energetic, sporty and young looking businessman at the casino roundabout near banks and the tax office finds no rest, since the tie of the coloured bronze figure has been stolen again and again as well as the black briefcase which he has placed next to him. The Belgian sculptor and conceptual artist Guillaume Bijl, born in Antwerp in 1946, was a professor at the Münster Art Academy from 2001 to 2011. His humorous figure was donated by the Sparda Bank West to the city of Wuppertal in 2007 which placed it on a 1.4 metre high black pedestal. "Schwarzer Fleck" (black spot) is the name of the square because it received a dark asphalt surface after realignment of the intersection. The sculpture is called "Tie Man" but the name chosen by the artist, "A New Successful Day", indicates its symbolic meaning.

Tippen Tappen Tönchen

Die Wuppertaler lieben ihre vielen Treppen, weil sie direkt und schnell von den Höhen in die Stadt führen. Von den klappernden Schuhabsätzen auf den Treppenstufen leitet sich der Name der Tippen-Tappen-Tönchen-Treppe her. Sie führt von der Straße Am Kasinogarten im Luisenviertel in 103 Stufen zur 16 Meter höher liegenden Gertrudenstraße am Ölberg mit seinem alten Arbeiterviertel. Ihr Verlauf ist verwinkelt. Von ihren Absätzen hat man schöne Ausblicke auf die Stadt.

Tippen Tappen Tönchen

The people in Wuppertal love their many stairs because they lead from the heights into the city directly and quickly. The name of the Tippen- Tappen- Tönchen staircase derives from the rattling shoe heels on the stairs. It leads from the street Am Kasinogarten to the Luisen district in 103 steps to the16 metres higher lying Gertruden Street on the Ölberg with its old working class neighbourhood. The course is angled. One has beautiful views of the city from its platforms.

Panoramablick vom Ölberg über das Luisenviertel zu den Elberfelder Südhöhen

Türme prägen die Blicke vom Ölberg auf die Elberfelder Südhöhen. Von links nach rechts ist das Turmpaar der klassizistischen Katholischen Kirche St. Laurentius aus dem Jahr 1847 zu sehen. Der Düsseldorfer Baurat Adolph von Vagedes, ein Schinkel-Schüler, war ihr Architekt. Über den weiten Bogen des Schwebebahngerüsts bei der Brücke Ohligsmühle sind die Türme der Historischen Stadthalle fast von den Parkbäumen verborgen. Neben dem Hotelneubau sieht man die „Schwimmoper". Dieses moderne Hallenbad aus dem Jahr 1957 wurde durch den Wuppertaler Baudezernenten Friedrich Hetzelt (1903-1986) errichtet. Das Städtische Bad erhielt seinen humorvollen Spitznamen, nachdem ein Jahr zuvor in Barmen das Opernhaus wieder aufgebaut wurde. Über ihrem konkav geschwungenen Dach erheben sich die Türme der neoromanischen Kirche St. Suitbertus. Sie wurde 1899 durch den Architekten Gerhard August Fischer errichtet, der auch den Wiederaufbau von Schloss Burg leitete. Darüber sind die Gebäude der Bergischen Universität zu sehen.

Panorama View from Ölberg over the Luisen District to the Elberfeld Südhöhen

Towers shape the view from Ölberg to the Elberfeld Südhöhen. From left to right: The pair of towers of the Classical Catholic Church of St. Lawrence from 1847 can be seen. The Dusseldorf architect Adolph von Vagedes, a Schinkel student, was the architect. The towers of the historic town hall are almost hidden by trees in the park over the broad arch of the suspension railway at Ohligsmühle bridge. One can see the "Schwimmoper" next to the new hotel building. This modern indoor swimming pool from 1957 was built by the Wuppertal Head of the Building Department Friedrich Hetzelt (1903-1986). The municipal swimming pool got its humorous nickname after the opera house in Barmen was rebuilt a year earlier. The towers of the neo-Romanesque church of St. Suitbertus rise above their concave roof. It was built in 1899 by the architect Gerhard August Fischer, who also led the reconstruction of Burg Castle. The buildings of Bergisch University can be seen above it.

Das Mahnmal für die Opfer des Nationalsozialismus in Wuppertal vor dem „De Weerth'schen Garten"

Tief von Schmerz gebeugt ist der Kopf unter den übereinander gebundenen Armen. 1958 stellte die Stadt Wuppertal diese Skulptur aus Muschelkalk vor den hohen, kahlen Sockel des früheren Kaiser-Wilhelm-Denkmals. Der Bielefelder Bildhauer Herbert Volwahsen (1906-1988) schuf die eindrückliche Figur aus Muschelkalk. Sie ist ein Mahnmal für die Opfer des Nationalsozialismus. Inschriften auf den Seiten der Sockelmauer erinnern auch an das erste KZ im östlichen Stadtteil Kemna, das die Nationalsozialisten von 1933 bis 1934 einrichteten. Der kleine Park des „De Weerth'schen Gartens" ist ein Überrest des weitaus größeren „Lustgartens", den 1802 der wohlhabende Elberfelder Bankier Peter de Weerth (1767-1855) vor der damaligen Stadtgrenze zur Erholung durch den berühmten Landschaftsgärtner Friedrich Weyhe anlegen ließ. Im Hintergrund ist der achteckige Turm der „Sophienkirche", der Neuen Reformierten Kirche Elberfelds aus dem Jahr 1858 zu sehen.

Memorial for the Victims of National Socialism in Wuppertal in front of the "De Weert'schen Garden"

Deeply bowed by pain, the head is under the folded arms. The city of Wuppertal presented this sculpture made of shell limestone in front of the tall, bare pedestal of the former Kaiser Wilhelm monument in 1958. The Bielefeld sculptor Herbert Volwahsen (1906-1988) created the impressive figure out of shell limestone. It is a memorial for the victims of National Socialism. Inscriptions on the sides of the pedestal wall are also reminiscent of the first concentration camp in the eastern district of Kemna which the National Socialists established from 1933 to 1934. The small park of the "De Weerth'schen Garden" is a remnant of the much larger pleasure garden which the wealthy Elberfeld banker Peter de Weerth (1767-1855) had created for recreation by the famous landscape gardener Friedrich Weyhe outside the city boundary at that time. The octagonal tower of the "Sophien Church", the new reformed church of Elberfeld from 1858, is in the background.

Basilika St. Laurentius

Im streng evangelisch-reformierten Elberfeld mussten sich die wenigen Katholiken lange Zeit eine Kirche erkämpfen. Auf dem Grundstück des heutigen Von der Heydt-Museums konnten sie von 1683 bis 1737 in einer Kapelle Messen feiern. Danach erhielten sie eine neue Kirche an der Burgstraße. Nachdem aber die Katholische Pfarrgemeinde auf 4 500 Gläubige durch Zuzug von Fabrikarbeitern und Handwerkern erheblich gewachsen war, musste eine größere neue Kirche gebaut werden. Die Katholiken stellten nun fast ein Viertel der insgesamt 24 000 Elberfelder. 1828 wurde auf dem Osterfeld, dem heutigen Laurentiusplatz, der Grundstein gelegt; 1835 wurde sie eingeweiht. Ihr Architekt war der Schinkelschüler Adolph von Vagedes (1777-1842), der die Kirche im damals bevorzugten klassizistischen Stil plante. Die beiden Türme mit ihren schlanken oktogonalen Dächern und hohen Spitzen sind ein Wahrzeichen der Stadt. Ihr Wiederaufbau nach dem Zweiten Weltkrieg dauerte von 1945 bis 1972. Sie erhielt eine reiche Ausmalung und Innenausstattung und steht seit 1984 unter Denkmalschutz. Neben der großen Orgel aus dem Jahr 1964 erhielt sie 1986 die älteste erhaltene Orgel in Wuppertal. Sie stammt aus der Werkstatt des Elberfelder Orgelbaumeisters Jakob Engelbert Teschemacher aus dem Jahr 1766.

St. Laurentius Basilica

The few Catholics in the strictly Protestant reformed Elberfeld had to fight for a church for a long time. They were able to celebrate mass in a chapel on the site of today's Von der Heydt Museum from 1683 to 1737. Then they received a new church on Burg Street. A larger church had to be built after the Catholic parish had grown considerably to 4,500 believers due to the influx of factory workers and craftsmen, however. Catholics now account for almost a quarter of the total of the 24,000 population of Elberfeld. The foundation stone was laid on the Osterfeld, today's Laurentiusplatz; it was inaugurated in 1835. Its architect was the Schinkel student Adolph von Vagedes (1777-1842) who planned the church in the classicist style that was preferred then. The two towers with their slender octagonal roofs and high spiers are a landmark of the city. Its reconstruction after the Second World War lasted from 1945 to 1972. It was given prolific painting and interior design and has been under monument protection since 1984. It received the oldest preserved organ in Wuppertal in 1986 in addition to the great organ from 1964. It comes from the workshop of the Elberfeld organ builder Jakob Engelbert Teschemacher from the year 1766.

Friedhofskirche an der Hochstraße

Bis 1850 konnten nur Mitglieder der Evangelisch-Reformierten Gemeinde in den Elberfelder Magistrat gewählt werden, obwohl Mitglieder anderer Konfessionen längst in der Überzahl waren. Als eine dritte Reformierte Kirche vor allem für die Bewohner der Nordstadt nötig wurde, sollte diese möglichst monumental werden, um an den ursprünglichen Vorrang der Reformierten zu erinnern. Für diese „reformierte Antwort auf den Bau der katholischen Laurentiuskirche" überzeugte der Entwurf des Berliner Architekt Johannes Otzen (1839-1911). Im Stil der Neoromanik erhielt die Kirche einen quadratischen, nicht durch Schiffe unterteilten Innenraum unter einem 20,5 Meter hohen Sterngewölbe, darüber der beherrschende Vierungsturm mit achtseitigem Turmhelm. Dieser ist nahezu von der ganzen Stadt sichtbar. Sie wurde 1898 eingeweiht. Die Kirche erhielt eine reiche Ausstattung und besitzt auch heute noch, nach etlichen Restaurierungen und Ergänzungen, eine Sauerorgel von 1898. Sie dient bis heute als Gemeinde- und Friedhofskirche.

Cemetery Church on Hoch Street

Only members of the Evangelical Reformed Church could be elected to the Elberfeld Municipal Administration until 1850 although members of other denominations were already in the majority. When a third Reformed Church became necessary, especially for the inhabitants of Nordstadt, it was to be as monumental as possible in order to recall the original precedence of the Reformed Church. The design of the Berlin architect Johannes Otzen (1839-1911) proved convincing for this "reformed response to the construction of the Catholic Laurentius Church". The church was given a square, non-naval interior under a 20.5 metre high stellar vault in neo-Romanesque style with the dominant four-sided tower spire above it. It is visible from almost the whole city. It was inaugurated in 1898. The church was given rich furnishings and still has a Sauer organ from 1898 today after several restorations and additions. It still serves as a parish and cemetery church today.

Thomaskirche am Engelnberg

Ende des 19. Jahrhunderts entstand auf dem noch wenig bebauten Engelnberg im Norden der Stadt ein neuer Wohnbezirk, in dem die Lutherische Gemeinde Elberfeld 1909 ein Gemeindehaus baute. Architekt war Regierungsbaumeister Heinrich Plange, Baumeister war der bekannte Elberfelder Friedrich Cornehls (1864-1916), der 1911 auch das Gemeindehaus am Platz der Republik errichtete. Die Kirche ist im neobarocken Stil errichtet und erhielt, auch wenn sie als Gemeindehaus bezeichnet wurde, einen Turm mit geschweifter Haube an der Seite. Sie steht unter Denkmalschutz.

Thomas Church at Engelnberg

At the end of the 19th century a new residential area was built on the still sparsely built Engelnberg in the north of the city on which the Lutheran community of Elberfeld built a parish hall in 1909. The architect was government approved master builder Heinrich Plange, the builder was the well-known Friedrich Cornehls (1864-1916) from Elberfeld who also built the parish hall at the Platz der Republik in 1911. The church was built in the neo-Baroque style and although it was called a parish hall it has a tower with a cambered dome on the side. It is a listed building.

Schusterplatz

Arbeitersiedlung auf dem Ölberg

Als Anfang der 1970er Jahre durch Sanierung alter Wohnviertel vielfach Abriss von angeblich nicht mehr hygienischer Bausubstanz einsetzte, war es einer energisch auftretenden Initiative um Dr. Michael Metschies (1939-2000), dem Denkmalbeauftragten des Bergischen Geschichtsvereins, zu danken, dass die Stadt buchstäblich „wachgerüttelt" wurde, für die Erhaltung der alten, oft vom Bombenangriff nur wenig beschädigten Gebäude zu kämpfen. 1975 hatte das Denkmalschutzjahr Signalwirkung. Reichhaltige, oft verfallende Schmuckelemente des Historismus, die vor allem die Mietshäuser aus der Gründerzeit an den eng bebauten Straßen am Ölberg prägten, wurden neu entdeckt und nicht mehr als lästiges Beiwerk empfunden. Der Ölberg hat übrigens seinen Namen, weil es dort immer noch nur Öllampen gab, als längst in der Stadt die Elektrizität eingezogen war. Heute ist der einstmals als sozialer Brennpunkt empfundene Stadtteil ein lebendiges, multikulturelles Viertel geworden, das gerade durch die Atmosphäre der alten Häuser sehr beliebt ist.

Workers' Settlement on the Ölberg

It was thanks to an energetic initiative of Dr. Michael Metschies (1939-2000), memorial appointee of the Bergisch Historical Association, that the city was literally "shaken up" to fight for the preservation of the old buildings which had often only been slightly damaged by the bombing. The protection of historical building and monuments year in 1975 had a signalling effect. Rich often decaying decorative elements of historicism which particularly shaped the tenement buildings from the Wilhelminian era on the narrowly built streets on the Ölberg were rediscovered and no longer seen as an annoying accessory. Incidentally, Ölberg has its name because there were only oil lamps there long after electricity had entered the city. The district once felt to be a social hotspot has become a lively, multicultural district which is very popular today particularly due to the atmosphere of the old buildings.

Haus Noetzlin

Das größte, geschlossen in den historisierenden Baustilen der Gründerzeit errichte Viertel Europas findet sich in Elberfeld. An den Hängen des Nützenbergs und beim Bachtal der „Beek" bauten sich wohlhabende Elberfelder Familien ihre repräsentativen, oft schlossartigen Villen. Zahlreiche unter ihnen, wie die Villa Noetzlin im Jahr 1910, wurden nach Plänen des prominenten Elberfelder Architekten Heinrich Plange (1857-1942), auch Architekt der Thomaskirche am Engelnberg, errichtet. Neobarocke Bauelemente verbinden sich mit beliebten Schmuckformen der wilhelminischen Zeit. Mit dem klassizistischen Giebel über dem Säulenportal werden antike Formen zitiert. Die Villa steht seit 1992 unter Denkmalschutz.

Noetzlin House

The largest contained quarter in Europe that is built in the historicist styles of the Wilhelminian era can be found in Elberfeld. Wealthy Elberfeld families built their representative often castle like villas on the slopes of the Nützenberg and in the beck valley of the "Beek". Many of them, such as Villa Noetzlin in 1910, were built according to the plans of the prominent Elberfeld architect Heinrich Plange (1857-1942) who was also the architect of the Thomas Church on Engelnberg. Neo-Baroque building elements are combined with popular Wilhelminian style plasterwork. The classical gable of the pillared portal cites antique forms. The villa has been a listed building since 1992.

Haus Roseneck

Das Haus Roseneck ist eine schlossartige Villa im Briller Viertel Elberfelds. Der bekannte Elberfelder Architekt Carl Conradi (1874-1959) übernahm im Baujahr 1914 Elemente des „Heimatstils", um dieses neobarocke Gebäude mit hohem Walmdach zugleich repräsentativ zu gestalten und ihm trotzdem eine gewissen Bürgerlichkeit zu geben. Die Villa ist Blickpunkt an der Kurve der Goebenstraße und zeigt mit ihrem geschieferten Dachgeschoss regionalen Bezug.

Roseneck House

The Roseneck house is a castle like villa in the Brill district of Elberfeld. The well-known Elberfeld architect Carl Conradi (1874-1959) took over elements of the "Regional Traditional Style" in 1914, the year of construction, in order to make this neo-Baroque building with a high hipped roof appear representative at the same time and to give a certain middle class air nevertheless. The villa is a focal point on the curve of Goeben Street and shows regional reference with the slate structured attic.

Weyerbuschturm auf dem Nützenberg

Türme bauen macht nicht nur Kindern Spaß! Wie in einem Wettstreit entstanden auf den Höhen Wuppertals um die Jahrhundertwende vom 19. zum 20. Jahrhundert Türme. 1887 hatten die Barmer ihren Toelleturm bekommen. Elf Jahre später gründete der Elberfelder Knopffabrikant und Stadtrat Emil Weyerbusch (1846-1909) eine Stiftung zum Bau eines Turms auf dem fast 260 Meter hohen Nützenberg, an dessen Hängen sich das neue schöne Gründerzeitviertel Brill ausbreitet. Der Turm wurde schon 1898 fertig und ist 25 Meter hoch, vom Turmzimmer aus gelangt man zu einer Aussichtsplattform in 17 Meter Höhe.

Weyerbusch Tower on Nützenberg

Building towers is not only fun for children! Towers were constructed on the heights around Wuppertal at the turn of the century from the 19th to the 20th century as if in a competition. The people in Barmen got their Toelle Tower in 1887, the Elberfeld button manufacturer and city councillor Emil Weyerbusch (1846-1909) established a foundation eleven years later for the construction of a tower on the almost 260 metre high Nützenberg on whose slopes the new beautiful Wilhelminian district Brill spread. The tower was completed in 1898 and is 25 metres high, one goes from the tower room to a viewing platform at a height of 17 metres.

Von der Heydt-Turm auf der Königshöhe

Gegenüber des Nützenbergs, im Süden der Stadt auf der Königshöhe des 274 Meter hohen Kiesberg, hatte schon August von der Heydt, Schwager von Emil Weyerbusch und Initiator des Elberfelder Verschönerungsvereins, den 1892 errichteten Turm gestiftet. Er ist 20 Meter hoch und befindet sich mitten im Waldgelände der Königshöhe, auf der die Familie eine große Villa als Sommersitz besaß. Diese konnte 1980 vom Abriss gerettet werden und ist heute ein Haus der Kunst und Künstler. Der Turm erinnert an Türme mittelalterlicher Burganlagen, er hat einen auffallend großen Erker in elf Meter Höhe.

Von der Heydt Tower on Königshöhe

August von der Heydt, brother-in-law of Emil Weyerbusch and initiator of the Elberfelder Beautification Association, donated the tower built opposite the Nützenberg in the south of the city on the Königshöhe of the 274 metres high Kiesberg in 1892. It is 20 meters high and is located in the middle of the forest area of the Königshöhe where the family owned a large villa as a summer residence. This could be saved from demolition in 1980 and is a house for art and artists today. The tower is reminiscent of towers of medieval castles; it has a strikingly large bay which is eleven metres high.

Blick hinter die Kulissen von Radio Wuppertal am „Tag der offenen Tür" während „Wuppertal 24h live"

Am 6. Oktober 1991 startete Radio Wuppertal, der private Lokalsender. Radio Wuppertal ist das meistgehörte Radioprogramm in Wuppertal. Gesendet wird über die UKW-Frequenz 107,4 vom Sender am Westfalenweg. Außerdem ist Radio Wuppertal über das Internet und über Apps via Smartphones und Tablets hören. Seit Beginn hat die Redaktion zahlreiche Hörfunk-Preise erhalten.

A look behind the scenes at Radio Wuppertal on the "Open Day" during "Wuppertal 24h live"

Radio Wuppertal, the private local station, started on October 6, 1991. Radio Wuppertal is the most listened to radio station in Wuppertal. It is broadcast on the FM frequency 107.4 from the station on Westfalenweg. Radio Wuppertal can be heard via the internet and on apps via smartphones and tablets in addition. The editors have received numerous radio awards since its inception.

Bayer-Werk

Die Schwebebahn fährt mitten durch das Gelände des Bayer-Werks in Elberfeld. Gebäude und Röhrensysteme geben dem Westrand des Stadtteils ihr Gepräge. Bis heute arbeiten hier mehr als 1 000 Mitarbeiter des weltberühmten Chemie- und Pharmariesens. Seine Keimzelle war allerdings in Heckinghausen, wo der Kaufmann Friedrich Bayer (1825-1880) und der Färber Johann Friedrich Weskott (1821-1876) eine kleine chemische Fabrik gründeten und dort die Farbstoffe Fuchsin und Anilin produzierten. 1866 war das Unternehmen so groß geworden, dass es im Westen Elberfelds, im Stadtteil Varresbeck, an der Wupper einen neuen Standort erhielt. Von hier aus wurde 1895 das Werk für die Produktion in Wiesdorf, ein Stadtteil des späteren Leverkusen auf den Rheinwiesen gegründet. Zunächst blieben Forschung und Verwaltung in Elberfeld; hier erforschte der Nobelpreisträger Gerhard Domagk die Anwendung der Sulfonamide. Heute hat Bayer Health Care seinen Standort in Elberfeld, wo ca. 1 300 Menschen tätig sind. Das Aspirin, in Elberfeld entwickelt, trug den Namen Bayer in die Welt, heute werden in Wuppertal ca. 20 Wirkstoffe produziert.

Bayer Plant

The suspension railway runs right through the grounds of the Bayer plant in Elberfel Buildings and tube systems gave the western edge of the district its character. Mor than 1,000 employees of the world famous chemical and pharmaceutical company wor here to date. Its nucleus was in Heckinghausen, however, where the merchant Friedric Bayer (1825-1880) and the dyer Johann Friedrich Weskott (1821-1876) founded a sma chemical factory where they produced the dyes fuchsin and aniline. The company ha grown so large by 1866 that it was given a new location in the district of Varresbeck i the west of Elberfeld on the Wupper. The factory for production in Wiesdorf, a district o the later Leverkusen, was founded from here on the Rhine meadows in 1895. Researc and administration remained in Elberfeld initially. Nobel Prize winner Gerhard Domag explored the use of sulfonamides here. Bayer Health Care is based in Elberfeld toda where around 1,300 people work. The aspirin which was developed in Elberfeld carrie the name Bayer to the world; About 20 active ingredients are produced in Wupperta today.

Sonnborner Eisenbahnbrücke mit Schwebebahn

Drei Verkehrsmittel zugleich treffen häufig in Sonnborn zusammen. Über die Brücke aus dem Jahr 1882 fahren die Eisenbahnzüge der Strecke Wuppertal-Düsseldorf, unter ihr fährt die Schwebebahn, unter dieser wiederum die Kraftfahrzeuge auf der alten Bundesstraße 7. Die Brücke ist immer ein beliebtes Fotomotiv, sie zeigt auch, wie eng und deshalb kompliziert das Tal der Wupper für die Verkehrsführungen ist.

Sonnborn Railway Bridge with Suspension Railway

Three means of transport meet in Sonnborn at the same time. The railway lines of the Wuppertal Dusseldorf line run over the bridge which is from 1882, the suspension railway runs underneath it and the motor vehicles of the old federal highway 7 pass underneath. The bridge is always a popular photo subject; It also shows how narrow and therefore complicated the valley of the Wupper is for the traffic routes.

Märchenbrunnen im Zooviertel

1897 erhielt die Stadt Elberfeld ein üppiges Geschenk. Die Architekten Rudolf Hermanns und Kuno Riemann, die beim Aufbau des schönen, neuen Wohnviertels am Zoo maßgeblich beteiligt waren, ließen für 23 000 Mark am kleinen Platz der Wotanstraße den Märchenbrunnen errichten. Sie entwarfen ihn selbst und ließen ihn dann bei dem Kölner Bildhauer Wilhelm Albermann als Zinkguss fertigen. Zu jedem Zoobesuch gehört der Abstecher zum Märchenbrunnen, um dort die Figuren aus den bekanntesten Märchen Aschenputtel, Dornröschen, Rotkäppchen und Schneewittchen der Brüder Grimm zu bestaunen. 2006 konnte er durch Bürgerspenden und Mittel der NRW-Stiftung restauriert werden. Seitdem füllen sich die von den Nationalsozialisten entfernten Wasserbecken wieder regelmäßig. Bei Dunkelheit ist der Brunnen beleuchtet.

Fairytale fountain in the Zoo Quarter

The city of Elberfeld received a lavish gift in 1897. The architects Rudolf Hermanns and Kuno Riemann who were instrumental in the construction of the beautiful, new residential district at the zoo had the fairy tale fountain built for 23,000 marks on the small square on Wotanstraße. They designed it themselves and then had it made as a zinc casting by the Cologne sculptor Wilhelm Albermann. The detour to the fairy tale fountain to admire the characters from the most famous fairy tales, Sleeping Beauty, Little Red Riding Hood and Snow White of the Brothers Grimm is a must for every visitor to the zoo. It was restored due to citizens` donations and funding from the NRW Foundation in 2006. The pools removed by the National Socialists have regularly filled up again since then. The fountain is illuminated when it is dark.

Bahnhof Zoo

Das neue Villenviertel beim 1881 eröffneten Zoo Elberfeld bekam einen Haltepunkt der Eisenbahnlinie nach Düsseldorf. Von außerhalb kamen immer mehr Touristen ins schöne Viertel, so dass 1898 ein fast märchenhaft anmutendes Bahnhofsgebäude über mehrere Etagen gebaut wurde. Von der Empfangshalle im oberen Bereich erreicht man über ein Sockelgeschoss die viel tiefer liegenden Bahnsteige. In Fachwerkbauweise errichtet mit weit überkragenden Walmdächern und seinem hübschen Turm ist dieser Bahnhof sehenswert. 1987 wurde er unter Denkmalschutz gestellt. Seit 1988 hält nur noch die S-Bahn hier, die Bahnsteige für die Fernverbindungen wurden abgebaut. 2012 brannte der Dachstuhl aus, aber das Gebäude konnte wieder restauriert werden. Im Bahnhof Zoo befindet sich ein Restaurant.

Zoo Station

The Elberfeld Zoo was opened in 1881 and gained a stopping point on the railway line to Dusseldorf. As increasing numbers of tourists came to the beautiful quarter from outside the area an almost fairy tale like station building was built over several floors in 1898. The much lower platforms can be accessed from the lobby in the upper area via a base level. This station built as a half-timbered construction with wide extended hipped roofs and its pretty tower is worth seeing. It became a listed building in 1987. Only the suburban railway has stopped here since 1988, the platforms for the long distance connections have been dismantled. The attic burned out in 2012 but the building was restored. There is a restaurant at the Zoo Station.

Zoologischer Garten

Nicht so sehr die Tiere, sondern das Vergnügen waren früher der Hauptgrund für das Publikum den Zoo zu besuchen. So eröffnete er 1881 mit gerade 34 Tieren, darunter zwei Wölfe und ein Bär. 1879 hatten die Elberfelder eine Aktiengesellschaft zum Aufbau eines Zoologischen Gartens gegründet und ihm ein repräsentatives Empfangsgebäude im Kolonialstil errichtet. Damals konnte man auf dem See Kahn fahren. Heute dient er vielen Wasservögeln als Quartier und der Gibbon-Familie als Schwing- und Sprungrevier. 1937 übernahm die Stadt Wuppertal den Zoo, nun wurde er wissenschaftlich weiter ausgebaut. Heute leben etwa 4 000 Tiere aller Arten hier und der Wuppertaler gehört zu den attraktivsten Zoos in Deutschland, vor allem wegen seiner landschaftlichen Lage. 1995 wurde die neue Elefantenanlage errichtet, der heute eine achtköpfige Elefantenherde mit ihren fast alljährlich geborenen Nachwuchs lebt. Ein Höhepunkt war 2006 die Pinguinale, zu der in der ganzen Stadt individuell bemalte und gestaltete große Kunststoffpinguine aufgestellt waren, um in einem langen Zug zum Zoo transportiert zu werden zur Feier des 125jährige Bestehens. Heute sind sie überall als ein Wuppertaler Identitätszeichen in der Stadt zu finden.

Zoological Garden

Pleasure used to be the main reason for the public to visit the zoo and far less the animals. It thus opened in 1881 with just 34 animals including two wolves and a bear. The people in Elberfeld founded a corporation to build a zoological garden and built a representative reception building in colonial style in 1879. At that time you could sail on Lake Kahn. It is used by many waterfowl as living quarters and by the Gibbon family as a swinging and jumping area today. The city of Wuppertal took over the zoo in 1937 which has now been developed further scientifically. About 4,000 animals of all kinds live here today and the Wuppertal Zoo is one of the most attractive in Germany particularly because of its scenic location. The new elephant enclosure in which an eight headed herd of elephants with their offspring, which are born nearly every year, lives today was constructed in 1995. The Penguinale celebrating the 125th anniversary where individually painted and designed large plastic penguins were set up throughout the city to be transported in a long train to the zoo was a highlight in 2006. They can be found everywhere in the city today as a sign of Wuppertal identity.

Evangelische Hauptkirche Sonnborn und Stadion am Zoo

Einer der ältesten Kirchorte im Wuppertal ist Sonnborn, das wohl in vorchristlicher Zeit einen heiligen Brunnen hatte. Zwischen dem 6. und 9. Jahrhundert entstand hier die erste Sonnborner Kirche. Sie gehörte zum Besitz des Klosters Gräfrath, 1539 wurde der erste protestantische Pfarrer nach Sonnborn berufen. Nach den beiden Vorgängerkirchen wurde 1926 auf dem Felsplateau über der sich nach Süden wendenden Wupper die neue, beeindruckende Hauptkirche errichtet. Der Provinzialkirchenbaumeister Arno Eugen Fritsche (1858-1939) errichtete sie in einem Misch-Stil aus neobarocken Formen des Heimatstils und Art-Déco-Elementen. Sie hat eine prächtige Innenausstattung und ist ein herausragendes Beispiel des Kirchenbaus der 1920der Jahre. 2007 erhielt der Glasraum, der im Inneren von dem Braunschweiger Architekturbüro Ahad als Familienkirche eingebaut wurde, den 1. Preis der Auszeichnung guter Bauten des Bundes Deutscher Architekten.

Am Südufer, direkt an das Zoogelände angrenzend, befindet sich das Stadion am Zoo. Im Oktober 1924 wurde es eröffnet als „Bergisches Stadion" für 38 000 Besucher und galt als das größte und modernste Stadtion Westdeutschlands. Seine frühere Radrennbahn war berühmt. Errichtet von den Kölner Architekten Theo Nussbaum und Theo Wilkens wurde es wegen des typischen Art Déco-Stils vor allem seines Eingangsgebäudes 1983 unter Denkmalschutz gestellt. Heute wird es vom Wuppertaler SV genutzt.

Sonnborn Evangelical Main Church and Arena at the Zoo

One of the oldest places of worship in Wuppertal is Sonnborn which probably had a holy well in pre-Christian times. The first Sonnborn church was built here between the 6th and 9th century. It belonged to the possessions of the Gräfrath monastery, the first Protestant pastor was called to Sonnborn in 1539. The new, impressive main church was built in 1926 on the rocky plateau above the south facing Wupper after there had been two predecessor churches. Its architect was the provincial church architect Arno Eugen Fritsche (1858-1939) whose design was a mixture of neo-Baroque forms of home style and Art Deco elements. It has a magnificent interior design and is an outstanding example of 1920s church architecture. The glass room by the Braunschweig architecture office Ahad which was installed inside as a family church in 2007 received the 1st prize of the award Good Buildings from the Association of German Architects in 2007.

The stadium at the zoo is on the south bank, directly bordering on the zoo. It was opened as "Bergisch Stadium" for 38,000 visitors in 1924 and was considered the largest and most modern stadium in West Germany. Its former cycle track was famous. Built by the Cologne architects Theo Nussbaum and Theo Wilkens it was listed as a historic monument in 1983 because of the typical Art Deco style, particularly in its entrance building. Today it is used by Wuppertal SV.

Vohwinkler Flohmarkt

In Sonnborn verlässt die Schwebebahnstrecke den Wupperlauf und führt weiter nach Westen zum Stadtteil Vohwinkel. Dort lockte seit seinem Beginn in den 1970er Jahre der alljährliche Trödel- und Flohmarkt unter der Schwebebahn auf der Kaiserstraße bis zu 600 000 Besucher an und kam deshalb auch in das Guinness-Buch der Rekorde. Organisiert wird er von der Arbeitsgemeinschaft Vohwinkler Vereine. Es gab sogar Sonderpostämter der Deutschen Bundespost zum Flohmarkttermin. Nach dem tragischen Unglück bei der Love-Parade in Duisburg konnten Verein und Stadt nicht mehr die erhöhten Sicherheitsauflagen für Massenveranstaltungen aufbringen. Deshalb fiel der Flohmarkt 2012 zum ersten Mal in seiner Geschichte aus, in den Folgejahren fand er bis 2018 wieder statt. 2019 musste er wegen finanzieller Probleme noch einmal ausfallen. In Vohwinkel wird er jedoch auch für die Zukunft weiter geplant.

Vohwinkel Flea Market

The suspension railway line leaves the course of the Wupper in Sonnborn and continues west to the Vohwinkel district. The annual junk and flea market under the monorail on Kaiser Street has attracted up to 600,000 visitors since it began in the 1970s and was therefore also included in the Guinness Book of World Records. It is organized by the Vohwinkel Working Group Association. There were even special post offices from the German Federal Post on flea market days. The city and association could no longer summon up the increased safety requirements for mass events after the tragic Duisburg Love Parade disaster. The flea market did not take place in 2012, therefore, for the first time in its history, it took place again in the following years until 2018. It had to be cancelled again in 2019 because of financial problems. Plans are also being made for the future in Vohwinkel, however.

Kaiserwagen in der Schwebebahnwerkstatt

Zur Jungfernfahrt der Schwebebahn am 24. Oktober 1900 fuhr Kaiser Wilhelm II. mit Kaiserin Auguste Viktoria und seinem Gefolge von Döppersberg (heute Hauptbahnhof) bis Vohwinkel. Er benutzte dafür extra einen Salonwagen mit besonders gepolsterten Sitzen und Tischchen. Vor den Fenstern hingen goldfarbene Gardinen und mit Jugendstil-Ornamenten verzierte Glasscheiben dienten als Trennwände zwischen 1. und 2. Klasse. Dieser Wagen ist erhalten geblieben und wird nach immer neuen Restaurierungen und Reparaturen für Sonderfahrten eingesetzt. Die können gebucht werden, nicht nur für die Stadtrundfahrt, sondern auch, um Hochzeit zu feiern oder einfach mit Freunden gemütlich Kaffee zu trinken.

Kaiser Carriage in the Suspension Railway Workshop

Kaiser Wilhelm II rode with Empress Auguste Viktoria and his entourage from Döppersberg (the main railway station today) to Vohwinkel on the maiden voyage of the suspension railway on October 24, 1900. He used an extra saloon carriage with especially upholstered seats and small tables. Gold coloured curtains hung in front of the windows and glass panes adorned with Art Nouveau ornaments served as partitions between the 1st and 2nd class. This carriage has been preserved and is used for special trips after restoration and repairs. It can not only be booked for a city tour, but also to celebrate a wedding or simply to have a coffee with friends.

Rathaus Vohwinkel

Malerisch nannte man den Stil, der Elemente des Historismus mit fantasiereichem Erker und Turmformen kombinierte. Es sollte auch heimatlich, altstädtisch wirken. Am Rand der äußerst fruchtbaren Mettmanner Börde mit ihren Lößböden war Vohwinkel von 1877 bis 1929 ein eher ländlich geprägter Verwaltungssitz des Kreises Mettmann. 1898 wurde das Rathaus der Stadt Vohwinkel für Gemeinderat, Verwaltung und Sparkasse eingeweiht. Vohwinkel selbst wurde erst 1921 als Stadt anerkannt. Nur für wenige Jahre, denn 1929 kam es zur neuen Großstadt Wuppertal. Mit den ländlichen Orten, aber auch von Kalksteinabbau geprägten Orten Dönberg, Dornap, Obensiebeneick und Schöller hat es heute ca. 30 000 Einwohnern und ist der drittgrößte Stadtteil Wuppertals.

Vohwinkel Town Hall

The style that combines elements of historicism with imaginative bays and tower forms is called pictorial. It should also look native, old-town. Vohwinkel, situated at the edge of the extremely fertile Mettmanner Börde with its loessial soils, was a rather rurally characterised administrative headquarters of the district of Mettmann from 1877 to 1929. The city hall of the City of Vohwinkel was inaugurated for the local council, administration and the savings bank in 1898. Vohwinkel itself was only recognized as a city in 1921, but only for a few years as it was incorporated into the new city of Wuppertal in 1929. It has about 30,000 inhabitants today with the rural towns, but also from the mining places Dönberg, Dornap, Obensiebeneick and Schöller which are characterised by limestone, and is the third largest district in Wuppertal.

Bahnhof Vohwinkel

Vor allem als Eisenbahnknotenpunkt ist Vohwinkel seit dem 19. Jahrhundert bekannt. Hier stoßen drei Bahnlinien aufeinander. Neben den beiden Linien, die von Düsseldorf durch Wuppertal geführt wurden, geht von hier aus eine Linie nach Essen. Im Südosten schloss sich das Gelände eines großen Güter- und Verschiebebahnhofs an. 1841 wurde Vohwinkel von der Düsseldorf-Elberfelder Eisenbahngesellschaft in Betrieb genommen. Das heutige Bahnhofsgebäude wurde 1908 errichtet, aber seit 1990 nicht mehr genutzt. 1991 wurde die Nordbahn, eigentlich Rheinische Strecke geschlossen, seit 2006 wurde sie als Nordbahntrasse, also Fahrrad- und Fußweg eröffnet. Von Vohwinkel aus hat sie Anschluss an den Panoramaweg nach Neviges und Essen. Vohwinkel ist für den Personenverkehr nur noch ein Haltepunkt der S- und Regionalbahn. Seit 2008 hat der Bürgerverein Vohwinkel die ehrenamtliche Initiative „Bürgerbahnhof" gegründet. Nun ist der Vohwinkeler Bahnhof ein Ort für Ausstellungen, Konzert, Kunst, Kultur und Feste.

Vohwinkel Station

Vohwinkel has especially been known as a railway junction since the 19th century. Three railway lines formed a crossing here. A line goes to Essen from here in addition to the two lines which led from Düsseldorf through Wuppertal. The grounds of a large freight and shunting yard was added in the south east. Vohwinkel was taken into operation by the Düsseldorf-Elberfeld railway company in 1841. The present station building was built in 1908 but has not been in use since 1990. The northern railway was closed in 1991, but has been reopened as the Nordbahntrasse bicycle and footpath since 2006. It is connected to the panoramic trail to Neviges and Essen from Vohwinkel. Vohwinkel is only a stopping point for the suburban railway in terms of passenger transport. The Vohwinkel Civic Association has founded the volunteer initiative "Citizens Station". Vohwinkel train station is now a place for exhibitions, concerts, art, culture and festivals.

Schlosscafé
PAULANE

Schloss Lüntenbeck und das Atelier des Künstlers Martin Smida

Am Fuß eines Buchenwaldes, umgeben von drei Teichen, ist das im 16. und 17. Jahrhundert errichtete Herrenhaus eine Oase der Ruhe zwischen dem Industriegebiet Varresbeck und der A 46, von der Nordbahntrasse in wenigen Minuten zu erreichen. Urkundlich erwähnt wird der Hof Lüntenbeck im Jahr 1218 im Heberegister des Stiftes Gerresheim. Nach mehreren Besitzerwechseln kam das Gut in städtischen Besitz. 1971 übernahm der bekannte, 1927 geborene Lichtdesigner Johannes Dinnebier das Schloss, restaurierte im Laufe der folgenden 15 Jahre die verfallene Hofanlage und betrieb dort eine Manufaktur für Beleuchtungssysteme, die im Jahre 2019 aus Platzgründen nach Solingen-Gräfrath verlagert wurde. Wohnen, Gewerbe, Büros und Kultur sowie ein Restaurant sind in die wieder schönen, alten Gebäude eingezogen. Seit 1984 ist Schloss Lüntenbeck eingetragenes Baudenkmal. 24h Live ist die Gelegenheit, Wuppertaler Institutionen, Firmen und auch Künstlerateliers „von Innen" kennenzulernen. Auch Martin Smida öffnet dann sein Atelier am Schloss Lüntenbeck. Der 1960 geborene Bildhauer stammt aus Tschechien und studierte an der der Kunstakademie Düsseldorf. Er arbeitet vor allem aus Fundstücken skurrile Skulpturen, die immer wie Bewohner oder Wesen aus einer fantastischen surrealen Welt wirken, Humor und auch ein wenig unheimlich, sozusagen „gute Geister". Smida ist auch als Bühnenbildner tätig.

Lüntenbeck Castle and the Atelier of the Artist Martin Smida

The manor house built in the 16th and 17th centuries is an oasis of calm at the foot of a beech forest surrounded by three ponds between the Varresbeck industrial area and the A 46 and can be reached from Nordbahntrasse in a few minutes. Lüntenbeck court was first mentioned in a document in the register of the Gerresheim bar in 1218. The estate came into municipal ownership after several changes of ownership. The well-known, 1927 born- light designer Johannes Dinnebier took over the castle in 1971, restored the dilapidated court complex in the course of the following 15 years and operated a factory for lighting systems there which was relocated to Solingen-Gräfrath in 2019 due to a lack of space. Apartments, businesses, offices and culture as well as a restaurant have moved into the beautiful old buildings. Schloss Lüntenbeck has been a registered monument since 1984. 24h Live is the opportunity to get to know Wuppertal's institutions, companies and artist studios "from the inside". Martin Smida also opens his studio at Schloss Lüntenbeck. Born in 1960, the sculptor hails from the Czech Republic and studied at the Düsseldorf Art Academy. He uses humour to create bizarre sculptures that always look like inhabitants or creatures from a fantastic surreal world and also a little scary, "good spirits" - so to speak. Smida also works as a stage designer.

Rittergut Schöller

Im beliebten kleinen Ausflugsort Schöller im Tal der Düssel stehen die Reste einer alten Wasserburg, die 1182 urkundlich erwähnt wird. Das spätere Rittergut war ein Fronhof, der mit dem ganzen Dorf 1570 einem Brand zum Opfer fiel. Der Barmer Kaufmann Johann Peter Bredt (1756-1819) ließ es 1786 wieder aufbauen und übergab es seinem Sohn, dem in Düsseldorf ausgebildeten Maler Johann Peter Bredt (1782-1864), der auch als Kaufmann tätig war. Das Bild, das er von seiner Familie malte, ist im Besitz des Wuppertaler Von der Heydt-Museum. Der Turm der Evangelischen Kirche Schöller stammt aus dem 12. Jahrhundert.

Schöller Manor

The remains of an old moated castle which is mentioned in documents in 1182 are in the popular, small excursion location Schöller in the valley of the Düssel. The later manor was a tournament yard which fell victim to fire in 1570 together with the whole village. The Barmer merchant Johann Peter Bredt (1756-1819) had it rebuilt in 1786 and handed it over to his son, the Düsseldorf trained painter Johann Peter Bredt (1782-1864) who also worked as a merchant. The picture he painted of his family is owned by the Wuppertal Von der Heydt Museum. The tower of the Evangelical Church in Schöller dates back to the 12th century.

Manuelskotten im Kaltenbachtal

Den harten Beruf des Knieschleifers kann man noch im Manuelskotten kennenlernen. Der unter Denkmalschutz stehende, vom Wasser des Kaltenbachs betriebene Kotten ist der letzte seiner Art in Wuppertal. Beim Knieschleifen werden große Messerklingen mit dem Knie gegen den mächtigen Schleifstein gedrückt, eine Methode, die feinste Schliffe herstellt. Der Manuelskotten liefert bis heute Schleifarbeiten für die Industrie. Für ein Remscheider Unternehmen schleift er große Cuttermesser für fleischverarbeitende Maschinen. 2006 konnte mit Mitteln der Regionale sein Wasserrad ersetzt werden. Wer mit der historischen Straßenbahn vom Museum in Kohlfurth nach Cronenberg herauffährt, kommt auf dem schönen Wanderweg zurück am Schleifkotten vorbei.

Manuelskotten in Kaltenbachtal

You can still get to know the hard profession of the knee grinder in Manuelskotten. The listed grinding mill, operated by the water from the Kaltenbach stream, is the last of its kind in Wuppertal. Large knife blades are pressed with the knee against the powerful whetstone when kneeling, a method that produces the finest cuts. Manuelskotten supplies the grinding work industry today. It grinds large craft knives for meat processing machines for a company from Remscheid. It was able to replace its water wheel in 2006 due to funds from the Regionale. If you take the historic tram from the museum in Kohlfurth to Cronenberg you will come back to the grinding mill on the beautiful hiking trail.

Das Straßenbahnmuseum Kohlfurth

29 ausgemusterte Straßenbahnen sind in der Halle des Straßenbahnmuseums an der Kohlfurth im Tal der Wupper westlich von Cronenberg zu sehen. Von 1874 bis 1987 gab es im Bergischen Land viele Straßenbahnlinien, die nach und nach zu Gunsten von Busverbindungen aufgegeben wurden. Der 1969 gegründete Verein Bergische Museumsbahnen e.V. baute das Museum mit seiner Werkstatt seit 1971 auf, um die Erinnerung an das beliebte Verkehrsmittel zu erhalten. Im Sommer fährt an jedem zweiten Wochenende eine Linie parallel zum Kaltenbachtal den steilen Berg nach Cronenberg hinauf. Sie hat auf der Strecke zwei Stationen für Spaziergänger. Alle Kinder freuen sich besonders, wenn es beim Abfahren lustig durch den Wald klingelt.

The Tram Museum in Kohlfurth

29 retired trams can be seen in the hall of the tram museum on the Kohlfurth in the valley of the Wupper west of Cronenberg. There were many tram lines in the country of Berg from 1874 to 1987 that were gradually abandoned in favour of bus services. The Bergisch Railway Museum Association, founded in 1969, has built up the museum with its workshop since 1971 in order to preserve the memory of the popular means of transport. A line runs parallel to the Kaltenbachtal up the steep mountain to Cronenberg every second weekend in the summer. There are two stations for hikers on the route. Children are especially happy as it amusingly rings through the woods during the descent.

TiC-Theater
BRILLEN

„Krings-Eck" und „An der Hütte" in Cronenberg

Das „Krings-Eck" in Cronenberg mit dem Blick auf das dreigeschossige Fachwerkhaus und den mit „welscher Haube" gekrönten Turm der Evangelisch-Reformierten Kirche hat den Charme alter bergischer Ortskerne bewahrt. 1050 wird „Krähen- oder „Kranichberg" schon erwähnt. Seit dem 14. Jahrhundert wurde hier in den Bergen Eisenerz abgebaut, das auch im Ort selbst verhüttet und geschmiedet wurde. Daran erinnert noch der Straßenname „An der Hütte". Nach einem verheerenden Stadtbrand 1829 erhielt der Ort zahlreiche Neubauten. Seit den 1970er Jahren hat der Cronenberger Heimatverein viele der alten Häuser vor dem Abriss gerettet und ihre Restaurierung veranlasst. Cronenberger Sicheln und Sensen waren in der ganzen Welt bekannt. 1929 kam Cronenberg zu Wuppertal.

"Krings-Eck" and „An der Hütte" in Cronenberg

The "Krings-Eck" in Cronenberg with its view of the three storey half-timbered building and the "Welscher Cap" crowned tower of the Evangelical Reformed Church have retained the charm of old Bergisch town centres. The "crows" or "crane mountain" had already been mentioned in 1050. Iron ore which was also smelted and forged in the village has been mined here in the mountains since the 14th century. The street name "An der Hütte" (ironworks) serves as a reminder of this. The town received numerous new buildings after a devastating city fire in 1829 and the Cronenberg Heimat Association has saved many of the old houses from demolition and restored them since the 1970s. Cronenberg sickles and scythes were known all over the world. Cronenberg joined Wuppertal in 1929.

Alte Schule in Cronenberg – heute Kulturhaus

Ganz nah sind die Zuschauer den Schauspielern auf den Bühnen des TIC in Cronenberg. Fast könnten sie mitspielen, und das macht den Reiz dieses beliebten Kammertheaters aus. Von 1831 bis in die 1960er Jahre besuchten Cronenberger Kinder die Schule hinter der Reformierten Kirche. Das leerstehende Gebäude wurde ein Kulturhaus für verschiedene kreative Gruppen und ein kleines Theater. Aus einer Kinderschauspielschule entstand 1986 durch den Theaterregisseur Ronald F. Stürzebecher mit begeisterten Laiendarstellern das immer professioneller arbeitende TiC Theater in Cronenberg. Es spielt heute unter der Leitung von Regisseur Ralf Budde und Musiker Stefan Hüffner in vier Spielstätten mitreißendes Kammertheater und hat eine eigene Schauspielschule. 25 000 Besucher im Jahr besuchen die Aufführungen.

Old School in Cronenberg – a Cultural Centre Today

The spectators are very close to the actors on the stages of the TiC in Cronenberg. They could almost play along and that is what makes this popular chamber theatre so appealing. Cronenberg children attended the school behind the Reformed Church from 1831 until the 1960s. The vacant building became a cultural centre for various creative groups as well as a small theatre. The drama director Ronald F. Stürzebecher created the increasingly professional working TiC Theatre in Cronenberg with its enthusiastic amateur actors from a children's drama school in 1986. It performs thrilling chamber theatre under the direction of director Ralf Budde and musician Stefan Hüffner in four venues today and has its own drama school. 25,000 visitors a year visit the performances.

Rollhockey RSC Cronenberg

Eine Hochburg des Rollhockeys ist Cronenberg seit der Gründung des RSC Rollschuh-Club Cronenberg im Jahr 1954. In Italien und südamerikanischen Ländern ist Rollhockey viel populärer als in Deutschland. Seit 1987 ist die Trainingshalle des RSC die weitgehend selbst finanzierte Alfred-Henckels-Halle an der Ringstraße. 2013 stand der Club auf Platz 25 der Weltrangliste des Rollhockeys. Bis heute spielt er in der 1. Liga Deutschlands und hat zahlreiche Meisterschaften und Pokalsiege errungen.

Roller Hockey RSC Cronenberg

Cronenberg has been a stronghold of roller hockey since the founding of the RSC Roller Skate Club Cronenberg in 1954. Roller hockey is much more popular in Italy and South American countries than in Germany. The training hall of the RSC has been the largely self-financed Alfred Henckels Hall on Ringstraße since 1987. The club ranked number 25 in the world ranking list of roller hockey in 2013. It still plays in the 1st German Division and has won numerous championships and cups to this day.

„Löckmann'sches" Haus in Küllenhahn

1977 ehrte die Stadt Wuppertal Rolf Löckmann mit dem Von-der-Heydt-Förderpreis, weil sich der bekannte Künstler und Denkmalschützer für die Erhaltung und Restaurierung historischer Bauten leidenschaftlich und ausdauernd eingesetzt hat. In den 1970er Jahren verschwand viel alte Bausubstanz, um Straßenbau und Neubauten zu weichen. Dabei hatte die Stadt gerade im Zweiten Weltkrieg viele schöne Gebäude durch die Bombenangriffe verloren. Durch das Engagement von Rolf Löckmann und Mitstreitern wie Dr. Michael Metschies begann ein Umdenken. Man begriff, wieviel Stadtatmosphäre gerade mit den alten Gebäuden verbunden ist. Rolf Löckmanns Fotografie half, das Bewusstsein für den Wert der alten bergischen Häuser zu wecken. Der „Häuserretter", wie er auch genannt wird, restaurierte das Fachwerkhaus im Ortsteil Küllenhahn, das vorher am Hahnerberg gestanden hat. Der „Gietenbruchsche Hof" musste dem Hahnerberg-Tunnel weichen. Er wurde an den Küllenhahn transloziert, wo Löckmann ihn in den folgenden acht Jahren wiederherstellte.

„Löckmann'sches" House in Küllenhahn

The city of Wuppertal honoured Rolf Löckmann with the Von der Heydt Prize in 1977 because the well-known artist and preservationist had worked passionately and perseveringly for preservation and restoration. A lot of old buildings had disappeared in the 1970s to give way to road construction and new buildings. The city had lost many beautiful buildings during the bomb attacks in World War II. A change of view began due to the commitment of Rolf Löckmann and colleagues such as Dr. Michael Metschies. One understood how much city atmosphere is currently connected with the old buildings. Rolf Löckmann's photography helped to raise awareness of the value of the old Bergisch houses. The "house rescuer", as he is also called, restored the half-timbered house in the district of Küllenhahn which had previously stood on the Hahnerberg. The "Gietenbruchsche Court" which was translocated to Küllenhahn where Löckmann restored it in the following eight years had to give way to the Hahnerberg tunnel.

Gelpetal

In den Tälern von Saalbach, der die Ronsdorfer Talsperre speist, Gelpe und Morsbach gab es bis ins 19. Jahrhundert mehr als 100 Schleifkotten und Schmieden, die alle ihre Energie aus der Wasserkraft bezogen. Im 5,8 Kilometer langen Gelpetal verschwanden Anfang des 20. Jahrhunderts nach und nach die Hammeranlagen und Stauteiche. Der Obere Jansenhammer war bis 1897 in Familienbesitz, wurde nach seinem Verkauf 1908 abgerissen. Nur der hohe Schornstein in seiner schönen achteckigen Form blieb stehen. 1993 wurde er als technisches Kulturdenkmal unter Schutz gestellt. Auf einer Wanderung durchs Gelpetal sind viele Reste der alten Industrieanlagen zu finden.

Gelpetal

There were more than 100 grinder workshops and forges in the valleys of the Saalbach which feeds the Ronsdorfer dam, Gelpe and Morsbach until the 19th century, all of which drew their energy from hydropower. The hammer installations and water retention basins in the 5.8 kilometre long Gelpetal gradually disappeared at the beginning of the 20th century. The Upper Jansenhammer was in family ownership until 1897 but was demolished after its sale in 1908. Only the tall chimney in its beautiful octagonal shape remained. In 1993 it was placed under protection as a technical cultural monument. Many remains of the old industrial plants are to be found on a hike through the Gelpetal.

Käshammer im Morsbachtal

Mit den Fördermitteln der Regionale 2006 konnte das 13 Kilometer lange Morsbachtal zwischen Wuppertal und Remscheid als „Erlebnisweg" erschlossen werden. Bis zum Anfang des 20. Jahrhunderts lieferte der in vielen Teichen gestaute Bach Energie für 42 Hammerwerke und 40 Schleifkotten, die verschiedene Werkzeuge für die ganze Welt produzierten. Heute sind Reste der einstigen Anlagen noch zu sehen. Beim Käshammer befand sich ursprünglich um 1607 eine Knochenmühle, 1824 wurde der Teich vergrößert, um die Wasserräder eines Schmiedehammers für Raffinierstahl zu betreiben. Ende des 19.Jahrhunderts wurde der Hammer stillgelegte, im Oberstock des Gebäudes zog eine Seidenweberei ein. Der Käshammer wurde ein beliebtes Ausflugslokal mit Schwimmbad und Kahnteich. Heute ist er in Privatbesitz und beispielhaft restauriert.

Käshammer in Morsbachtal

The 13 km long Morsbachtal between Wuppertal and Remscheid was opened up as an "adventure trail" with funding from the Regionale 2006. The stream, which was dammed in many basins, provided the energy for 42 hammer mills and 40 grinding workshops which produced various tools for the whole world. Remains of the former plants can still be seen today. A bone mill was originally located near the Käshammer around 1607, the pond was later enlarged in 1824 to operate the water wheels of a forging hammer for refining steel. The hammer works was shut down at the end of the 19th century and a silk weaving factory moved into the upper floor of the building. The Käshammer in Morsbachtal became a popular tourist restaurant with a swimming pool and a boating pond. Today it is privately owned and exemplarily restored.

Bandwirkerplatz
Volksbank
Franke

Bandwirkerplatz in Ronsdorf

„Ora et labora", Bete und Arbeite! Das war die Losung Ronsdorfer Bandwirker. Im 18.Jahrhundert spalteten sich radikal-pietistische Sektierer unter der Führung von Elias Eller (1690-1750) von der Evangelisch-Reformierten Kirche in Elberfeld ab und bauten südlich von Elberfeld in Ronsdorf eine eigene Siedlung, wo sie in Ruhe und ohne Glaubensstreit die Heimbandwirkerei betreiben konnten. Bis heute ist Ronsdorf ein Ort der Schmalbandwebereien. Besonders gut gelaunt waren die Bandwirker, wenn sie mit dem „Liewersack" voll mit Bändern beim Fabrikanten, der das ganze Material stellte, ihre Wochenproduktion abgeliefert hatten und mit Lohn nach Hause kamen. Dann war auch Zeit, einen Schwatz zu halten oder mit der Liebsten zu schäkern. Max Kratz (1921-2000), ein bekannter Bildhauer des 20. Jahrhunderts, in Remscheid geboren, schuf das humorvolle Bronze-Denkmal mit dem Bandwirkerpaar aus dem Jahr 1980 für den schönen Rasenplatz und Markt mitten in Ronsdorf vor dem Ämterhaus. Der Turm der Evangelisch-Lutherische Kirche Ronsdorf aus dem Jahr 1793, im Stil bergischer Hallenkirchen errichtet, ist im Bild zu sehen. Sie ist das älteste Kirchengebäude in Ronsdorf. die Kirche der Evangelisch Reformierten Gemeinde stammt aus dem Jahr 1858.

Bandwirkerplatz in Ronsdorf

"Ora et labora", pray and work! That was the slogan of the Ronsdorf bandweavers. Radical pietistic sectarians under the leadership of Elias Eller (1690-1750) split from the Evangelical Reformed Church in Elberfeld in the 18th century and built their own settlement south of Elberfeld in Ronsdorf where they could operate the small home band works quietly and without religious dispute. Ronsdorf is a place of narrow band weaving to this day. The band workers were in a particularly good mood when they delivered their weekly production with the "Liewersack" full of bands to the manufacturer who provided all the material and came home with payment. Then there was time to chat or flirt with your loved one. Max Kratz (1921-2000), a well-known sculptor of the 20th century, who was born in Remscheid, created the humorous bronze monument from 1980 with the band work couple for the beautiful lawn and market in the middle of Ronsdorf in front of the office building. The tower of the Evangelical Lutheran Church Ronsdorf from 1793, built in the Bergisch hall church style, can be seen in the picture. It is the oldest church building in Ronsdorf. The church of the Reformed Evangelical Community dates from 1858.

Ehemalige Städtische Grundschule in Ronsdorf

Lange Zeit hatte die Evangelisch-Reformierte Gemeinde von Ronsdorf, 1741 gegründet, noch keine Kirche. Die wurde erst 1858 errichtet und ist im Stil der neugotischen Schinkelkirchen gebaut. Doch ein Bet- und Schulhaus baute die Gemeinde schon 1742. 1828 wurde das heute unter Denkmalschutz stehende Fachwerkhaus als Schule mit Lehrerwohnung errichtet, bis 1868 kam der Anbau hinzu, so dass die Schule vier Klassenräume hatte. Sie ist das älteste erhaltene Schulgebäude von Ronsdorf, ein Stadtteil, der vor der Eingemeindung nach Wuppertal im Jahr 1929 eine selbständige Stadt im Landkreis Lennep war. Mit Unterbrechungen durch den 2. Weltkrieg wurde das Gebäude 1984 als Schule genutzt. Heute ist es sehr schön restauriert in Privatbesitz.

Former Municipal Primary School in Ronsdorf

The Evangelical Reformed Church of Ronsdorf, founded in 1741, did not have a church for a long time. It was first constructed in 1858 and is built in the style of neo-Gothic Schinkel churches. But the community had built a prayer and school house, as early as 1742. The half-timbered house, which is now a listed building, was built as a school with a teacher's flat in 1828 and the extension was added by 1868 so that the school had four classrooms. It is the oldest surviving school building in Ronsdorf, a district that was an independent town in the district of Lennep before incorporation into Wuppertal in 1929. The building was used as a school until 1984 with an interruption due to World War II. It is beautifully restored and in private ownership today.

Ronsdorfer Talsperre

Eine beispiellose Bürgerinitiative rettete die Ronsdorfer Talsperre. Ihre Mauer war in den 1990er Jahren so marode geworden, dass das Wasser abgelassen werden sollte. Bürger und der Förderverein „Ronsdorfer Talsperre e.V." erreichten, dass der Wupperverband die Talsperre von der Stadt Wuppertal übernahm und die Staumauer mit einer vorgesetzten, wasserundurchlässigen Betonschale auf der Staubeckenseite abdichtete. Die alte Hochwasserentlastung wurde erneuert. Heute ist die Mauer wieder begehbar und mit dem als Waldlehrpfad angelegten Uferweg verbunden. Die Ronsdorfer Talsperre wurde 1898 im Saalbachtal an der südwestlichen Ortsgrenze errichtet. Seit 1956 wird sie nicht mehr als Trinkwassersperre genutzt. Auch wenn die Staumauer erhalten ist, wurde ihr Wasserspiegel extrem gesenkt, da eine absolute Dichtigkeit der Mauer nicht mehr zu erreichen war. Im Flachwasserbereich der Sperre siedelte sich eine seltene Krebsart an. Der Edelkrebs Astacus lebt in in nährstoffreichen, sommerwarmen und niedrigen Gewässern in Wohnhöhlen unter den Wurzeln der im Uferbereich wachsenden Gehölze. Er wird bis zu 20 cm lang und ist heute durch Pilzerreger der „eingewanderten" Signalkrebse gefährdet.

Ronsdorf Dam

An unprecedented citizens' initiative saved the Ronsdorf dam. Its wall had become so dilapidated in the 1990s that the water was supposed to be drained. But a citizens' initiative and the support association "Ronsdorf Talsperre e.V." achieved that the Wupper Association took over the dam from the city of Wuppertal and sealed the dam with a superior, impermeable concrete shell on the reservoir side. The old spillway was renewed. Today, the wall is again accessible and connected to the forest path as a shore path. The Ronsdorf dam was built in 1898 in the Saalbachtal on the southwestern outskirts. It has no longer been used as a drinking water dam since 1956. Even though the dam has been preserved, its water level was lowered considerably, as an absolute impermeability of the wall was no longer achievable. A rare crab settled down in the shallow water area of the dam. The Astacus crayfish lives in nutrient rich, summer warmed and low waters in hole dwellings under the roots of the trees growing in the bank area. It is up to 20 cm long and is endangered by fungal pathogens of the "immigrant" signal crayfish today.

Lichtscheider Wasserturm und Herbringhauser Talsperre

Mit seiner Höhe von 58 Metern auf dem 350 Meter hohen Lichtscheid gilt der Lichtscheider Wasserturm als höchste Erhebung Wuppertals. 1975 errichtet, fasst er rund 1 540 Kubikmeter Wasser und versorgt die Stadtteile Ronsdorf, Bereiche Lichtscheids bis zur Unteren Lichtenplatzer Straße sowie Teile von Cronenberg.

Das Wasserwerk Herbringhausen bei der Herbringhauser Talsperre liefert ihm das Wasser. Diese 1900 errichtete Talsperre heißt auch die „Barmer Talsperre". Ihre gebogene Staumauer ist 33,5 Meter hoch und nach dem erfolgreichen „Intze-Modell" gebaut. Der Lüttringhauser Bürgermeister Richard Gertenbach hatte 1896 der Stadt Barmen Grundstücke auf Lüttringhauser Gebiet verkauft. Damit sicherte er die Trinkwasserversorgung für die eigene Stadt. Seit 1913 bezieht das Wasserwerk Herbringhausen auch Trinkwasser aus der Kerspe-Talsperre bei Wipperfürth, seit 1988 zusätzlich ein Kontingent aus der Großen Dhünn-Talsperre. Die westlichen Stadtteile Wuppertal erhalten Trinkwasser aus Rheinufer-Filtrat des Wasserwerks bei Düsseldorf-Benrath.

Lichtscheid Water Tower and Herbringhausen Dam

The Lichtscheid water tower is the highest elevation in Wuppertal with 58 metres and located on the 350 meter high Lichtscheid. It was built in 1975, holds about 1,540 cubic meters of water and supplies the districts of Ronsdorf, areas of Lichtscheid up to Untere Lichtenplatzer Street and parts of Cronenberg.

The Herbringhausen waterworks at the Herbringhausen dam provides it with water. This dam, built in 1900, is also called the "Barmen dam". Its curved dam wall is 33.5 metres high and built according to the successful "Intze design". The Lüttringhausen Mayor Richard Gertenbach had sold land in the Lüttringhauser area to the city of Barmen in 1896. He thus secured the drinking water supply for his own city. The waterworks Herbringhausen has also drawn drinking water from the Kerspe dam near Wipperfürth since 1913, in addition a contingent from the Great Dhünn dam since 1988. The western districts of Wuppertal receive drinking water from the Rhine bank filtrate of the waterworks near Düsseldorf-Benrath

Haus Cleff und Alte Kirche in Langerfeld

Schon 1922 „eignete" sich die Stadt Barmen den alten Ort Langerfeld an. Er war bis dahin eine selbständige Landgemeinde im westfälischen Kreis Schwelm, und viele Langerfelder haben sich lange Zeit eher als Westfalen denn Rheinländer gefühlt. 1304 wird Langerfeld urkundlich zum ersten Mal erwähnt. Der Ort war ein Zentrum des Eisenerz- und des Galmei-Abbaus, eines Zinkerzes, das auch große Fundstätten bei Schwelm hatte. Im 16. Jahrhundert entwickelte sich die Garnbleicherei. Später war Langerfeld vor allem ein Ort der Schmalbandwebereien. Das schöne alte Hofeshaus Cleff mit seiner hohen, verzierten Giebelseite errichtete 1680 Bauherr Johan Tönes. Er ließ einen Vierzeiler auf dem Türbalken einschnitzen: „Auf Gnad hab ich vertravet / und auf sein Wort dis Haus gebavet/ Der helfe mir das es werd volendt / zu seinem Lob und gutem Endt."

Jahrhundertelang mussten die Langerfelder zum Gottesdienst nach Schwelm wandern. 1766 trennten sie sich von der Mutterkirche und errichteten bis 1786 ihr erstes eigenes Gotteshaus. Die Alte Kirche Langerfeld entspricht den Gebäuden der bergischen Predigtkirchen, die mit ihren Emporen in einem rechteckigen hohen Hallenraum vielen Gemeindegliedern Platz geben sollten. Ihr Turm hat allerdings nicht eine dieser dicken „welschen" Hauben wie die Alte Kirche Wupperfeld, sondern ein schlichtes, einmal gefaltetes Pyramidendach.

Cleff Building and Old Church in Langerfeld

The city of Barmen "appropriated" the old town of Langerfeld as early as 1920. It had been an independent rural community in the Westphalian district of Schwelm until then and many inhabitants of Langerfeld had felt more Westphalian than Rhinelander for a long time. Langerfeld was mentioned in a document for the first time in 1304. The place was a centre of iron ore mining and calamine, a zinc ore, mining which also had large sites in Schwelm. Yarn bleaching developed in the 16th century. Langerfeld was a place of narrow band weaving more than anything. The builder Johan Tönes built the beautiful old Cleff court house with its high, decorated gable side. He had a quatrain carved into the door beam: "In grace I have entrusted / and built the house on his word / He help me that it would be done / to his praise and good end."

The inhabitants of Langerfeld had to go to the service in Schwelm for centuries. They separated from the mother church in 1766 and had built their first own church by 1786. The old Langerfeld church corresponds to the buildings of the Bergisch sermon churches which should provide space for many parishioners with their galleries in a rectangular high hall space. Its tower does not have one of these thick "welsch" hoods like the old church in Wupperfeld but a simple, once folded pyramid roof.

Bänderei Kafka in der ehemaligen Fabrik Kikuth an der Oeder Straße 47 und 49

Dicht gestreute Vergissmeinnicht-Blüten auf breiten Hosenträgern, ein kupferbraunes Rhombenmuster auf einer Herrenfliege - in der Bandweberei Kafka erobern sich alte Bandwirkertraditionen neue Plätze. Nicht mehr als schüchternes Wäsche- oder Namenband im Innern der Dessous versteckt, sondern als farbenfroher dekorativer modischer Akzent auf Blusen und Hemden, als formtragende Gestaltungsmittel auf schöner Tischwäsche, auf Tabletts, Taschen und Gardinen. 1991 übernahm die Textildesignerin Frauke Kafka die alte Bandfabrik von Friedel Mardey im alten Bandwirkerviertel Langerfeld. 2010 zog sie in ein altes, denkmalgeschütztes Gebäude der früheren Bandfabrik Kikuth bei dem früheren Tönnies-Bleicherhaus aus dem Jahr 1712. Hier produzieren nun die 25 mehr als 100jährigen hölzernen Jacquard-Bandstühle. Seit 2018 führt C. Pauli die Bänderei weiter. Ein Museum informiert über diese schöne alte Barmer Textiltradition und die Technik ihrer Herstellung. Mehr als 450 Muster umfasst das Sortiment der Bänderei. Die Bandweberei Kafka ist ein produzierendes Industriedenkmal und arbeitet für den Verkauf an Ort und Stelle und den Online-Shop. Im verschieferten Nachbarhaus aus dem Jahr 1853 werden im Ausstellungsraum Fülle und Vielfalt der schönen Bänder gezeigt.

Kafka Band Weaving in the Former Kikuth Factory, 47 and 49 Oeder Street

Densely scattered forget-me-not flowers on wide braces, a coppery brown rhombic pattern on a gentleman's tie - old band worker traditions conquer new places in the Kafka band weaving mill, no longer hidden as shy linen or a name band inside lingerie, but as a colourful decorative fashionable accent on blouses and shirts, as a formative design tool on beautiful table linen, on trays, bags and curtains. The textile designer Frauke Kafka took over the old band factory of Friedel Mardey in the old band weaver quarter of Langerfeld in 1991. In 2010 she moved to an old, listed building of the former Kikuth band factory at the former Tönnies bleacher building from 1712. 25 more than 100 year old wooden Jacquard band chairs are running here now. C. Pauli has continued the band weaving since 2018. A museum provides information about this beautiful old Barmen textile tradition and its production technique. More than 450 samples are included in the band weaving range. The Kafka band weaving mill is a manufacturing industrial monument and works for sales on site and also in the online store. The abundance and variety of beautiful bands are shown in the showroom in the slated neighbouring house which is from 1853.

Bleicherhaus Toennies an der Oehder Straße 51

Das Backsteinfabrikgebäude, das Kontor- und Wohnhaus aus dem 19. Jahrhundert und das wunderbar erhaltene alte Bleicherhaus bilden ein sehenswertes Ensemble nahe der Oehder Talbrücke der A1. 1712 ließ die Familie Tönnies das teilweise verschieferte Fachwerkhaus vierstöckig errichten. Im Dachgeschoss befanden sich die Lagerräume, auf der nordwestlichen Seite eine feuersichere Garnkammer, die auch vor Diebstahl schützte. Das Gebäude wurde 1984 unter Denkmalschutz gestellt. Durch das schon im Mittelalter übliche Garnbleichen, vor allem des Garns aus Flachs mit dem weichen, kalkarmen Wupperwasser war die Haupteinnahme-Quelle im Tal der Wupper von Heckinghausen über Barmen bis Elberfeld.

Tonnies Bleacher Building at Oehder Street 51

The brick factory building, the office and residential building from the 19th century and the wonderfully preserved old bleacher building near the Oehder Viaduct of the A1 form an ensemble that is worth seeing. The Tönnies family had the partially slated half-timbered house built over four floors in 1712. The storage rooms were in the attic, a fireproof yarn chamber on the northwest side also protected against theft. The building was made a listed building in 1984. Yarn bleaching with the soft, lime deficient water from the Wupper which was already common in the Middle Ages, especially of flax yarn, was the main source of income in the valley of the Wupper from Heckinghausen via Barmen to Elberfeld.

Beyenburger Stausee and Wupper mit Fischtreppe

Spitzwinklig biegt die Wupper bei dem Felsenplateau der Halbinsel Beyenburg in westliche Richtung ab. Vor dieser Biegung staut sie ein 8,6 Meter hoher Damm, der von 1898 bis 1900 zum Ausgleich der Wasserstandsregulierung gebaut wurde. Das hohe Wehr dieser Anlage bildete eine Sperre für den Fischaufstieg. Bis ins 20. Jahrhundert hinein war die Wupper eine Art Abwasserkanal für die vielen Fabriken an ihren Ufern. Umfassende ökologische Maßnahmen des Wupperverbandes haben seit den 1980er Jahren wieder Fischbestände geschaffen. Damit ihre Wanderungen an den Wehren nicht unterbrochen werden, richtete der der Wupperverband Fischtreppen ein. Der Beyenburger Fischaufstieg über einen mäandrierenden Bachlauf mit 55 Becken wurde 2012 fertig. Seitdem steigen auch die Lachse wieder in der Wupper auf.

Beyenburg Reservoir and Wupper with Fish Ladder

The Wupper bends westward at an acute angle along the rocky plateau of the Beyenburg peninsula. A 8.6 metre high dam, which was built from 1898 to 1900 to balance the water level regulation, jams it before this bend. The high weir of this plant formed a barrier to the ascent of fish. The Wupper was a sort of sewer for the many factories on its banks up until the 20th century. Comprehensive ecological measures by the Wupper association have been creating fish stocks since the 1980s. The Wupper association established fish ladders so that their migrations are not interrupted by the weirs. The Beyenburg fish ascent over a meandering creek with 55 pools was completed in 2012. The number of salmon in the Wupper has risen again since then.

Beyenburger Klosterkirche

An der Wupper in Beyenburg überquerte der alte Hanse- und Pilgerweg von Köln über Dortmund bis Nowgorod die Wupper. Sie war hier Grenzfluss zwischen dem Herzogtum Berg und der Grafschaft Mark. Beyenburg war ein Bergischer Amtssitz, zu dem das Gericht in Barmen, die Kirchspiele Lüttringhausen mit Ronsdorf, Remlingrade und Radevormwald gehörten. Um 1300 schenkte Engelbert I. von Berg das alte „Steinhaus" an der Wupperschleife dem flämischen Mönchsorden der Kreuzbrüder, die 1458 auf dem Beyenberg die spätgotische Kirche mit Dachreiter errichteten. Sehenswert sind ihr reich verziertes Chorgestühl und ein Hochaltar aus der Barockzeit mit dem Altargemälde der Rubens-Schule.
Das Orgelgehäuse stammt noch aus dem Jahr 1693. Nach der Säkularisierung durch Napoleon wurde das Kloster 1804 aufgehoben, 1963 kehrte der Kreuzherren-Orden nach Beyenburg zurück, Kirche und Klostergebäude wurden restauriert. Das Kloster vermietet seine schönen Säle für private Feste. Die Häuser des alten Beyenburger Kerns rund um die Klosterkirche haben ihr ursprüngliches Aussehen in bergischer Bauweise erhalten. Sehenswert ist ein Spaziergang durch Beyenburg, wo die Häuser an dem Steilhang über der Wupper so gebaut sind, dass sich die Haustüren im Obergeschoss befinden.

Beyenburg Monastery Church

The old Hanseatic and pilgrimage route from Cologne via Dortmund to Novgorod crossed the Wupper in Beyenburg. It was not the border river between the Duchy of Berg and the County of Mark here. Beyenburg was a Bergisch official residence which included the court in Barmen and the parish of Lüttringhausen with Ronsdorf, Remlingrade and Radevormwald. Engelbert I. von Berg gave the old "stone house" on the bow of the Wupper to the Flemish monks of the Order of the Cross around 1300, they built the late Gothic church with a ridge turret on Beyenberg in 1448. Its richly decorated choir stalls and a high altar from the Baroque period with the altarpiece from the Rubens School are worth seeing.
The organ case dates back to 1693. The monastery was repealed in 1804 after secularization by Napoleon, the Order of the Cross returned to Beyenburg in 1963, the church and monastery building were restored. The monastery rents out its beautiful rooms for private parties. The buildings of the old Beyenburg core around the monastery church have retained their original Bergisch architectural appearance. A walk through Beyenburg, where the houses are built on the steep slope above the Wupper so that the front doors are located on the upper floor, is worthwhile.

Impressum / Imprint

Wuppertal – Portrait einer Stadt
ISBN 978-3-96535-028-1

1. Auflage November 2019

klaes-regio Fotoverlag
Holger Klaes
Hünger 3, D-42929 Wermelskichen
http://klaes-regio.com eMail: post@klaes-w.de

Herausgeber und Fotografien:
Holger Klaes

Text:
Gisela Schmoeckel

Übersetzungen:
Joyce Nicholsen

Karte: Computerkartografie Carrle

Konzeption und Herstellung: Holger Klaes

Printed in Germany

Literaturverzeichnis / *Bibliography*

Boch, Rudolf, Das Bergische Land im 19. Jahrhundert (1814-1914) In: Geschichte des Bergischen Landes. Bd 2. Das 19. und 20. Jahrhundert. Bielefeld 2016. S. 171-267

de Bruyn-Ouboter, Hans-Joachim, 1200 Jahre Barmen. Wuppertal 2009. (Edition Köndgen)

Der Westdeutsche Impuls 1900 - 1914. Von der Heydt-Museum Wuppertal. 1984

Goebel, Klaus, Michael Knierim, Kurt Schnöring u. Volkmar Wittmütz, Geschichte der Stadt Wuppertal. Wuppertal 1977

Jung-Stilling, Johann Heinrich, Heinrich Stillings Jugend, Jünglingsjahre, Wanderschaft und häusliches Leben. Stuttgart, Reclam 1968, S. 204

Eschmann, Jürgen, Die Wuppertaler Schwebebahn, Geschichte, Technik, Kultur. Wuppertal 1990

Kitt, Roy, The Wupper Valley. Regionale 2006

Klaes, Holger u. Hans Joachim de Bruyn-Ouboter, Wuppertal, Die bergische Metropole. 3. Aufl. Wuppertal 2013 (Edition Köndgen)

Klaes, Holger u, Joachim Jäger, Wuppertal. Suchbildband. Wermelskirchen 2017 (FindeFuxx-Buch)

Schnöring, Kurt, Geschichte der Stadt Wuppertal. Kassel 2004

Langewiesche, Wilhelm, Elberfeld und Barmen. Barmen 1863

Lasker-Schüler, Else, Elberfeld im dreihundertjährigen Jubiläumsschmuck. In E.L.S., Der Prinz von Theben u. andere Prosa. Frankfurt Suhrkamp Taschenbuch, S. 163

Löckmann, Rolf und Michael Metschies, Wuppertal wiederentdeckt. 2. Aufl. 1975

Okroy, Michael, „...Damit die Träume atmen können". Vom Stadttheater Barmen zum Opernhaus Wuppertal. Wuppertal 2009

Pogt, Herbert, Historische Ansichten aus dem Wuppertal des 18. und 19. Jahrhunderts. 2. Aufl. 1988. (Bergischer Geschichtsverein - Abt. Wuppertal)

Reihe Wuppertals grüne Anlagen. Edition Köndgen, Bd 1 - 7

Schumann, Kerstin, Expedition³. Erlebnistouren und Ausflugsziele im Bergischen Städtedreieck. Regionale 2006 Agentur. Remscheid 200

Unser Ronsdorf. Historisches, Heiteres und Besinnliches. Verf. von Jolsua Halbach, Günter Konrad, Friedhelm Peters u.a. Wuppertal 1995

Kirchen und Gottesdienststätten in Wuppertal. Bd 1. Hrsg. von Klaus Goebel und Andreas Knorr. Bd 2. Hrsg. von Sigrid Lekebusch und Florian Speer. Bergischer Geschichtsverein Abt. Wuppertal. 2008

Hinweis auf die Zitate von Lasker-Schüler und Jean Cocteau im Vorwort finden sich bei Kurt Schnöring, „Wo die Wupper wuppert..." in: Jürgen Eschmann, Die Wuppertaler Schwebebahn. Wuppertal 1990. S. 219-228

Wikipedia

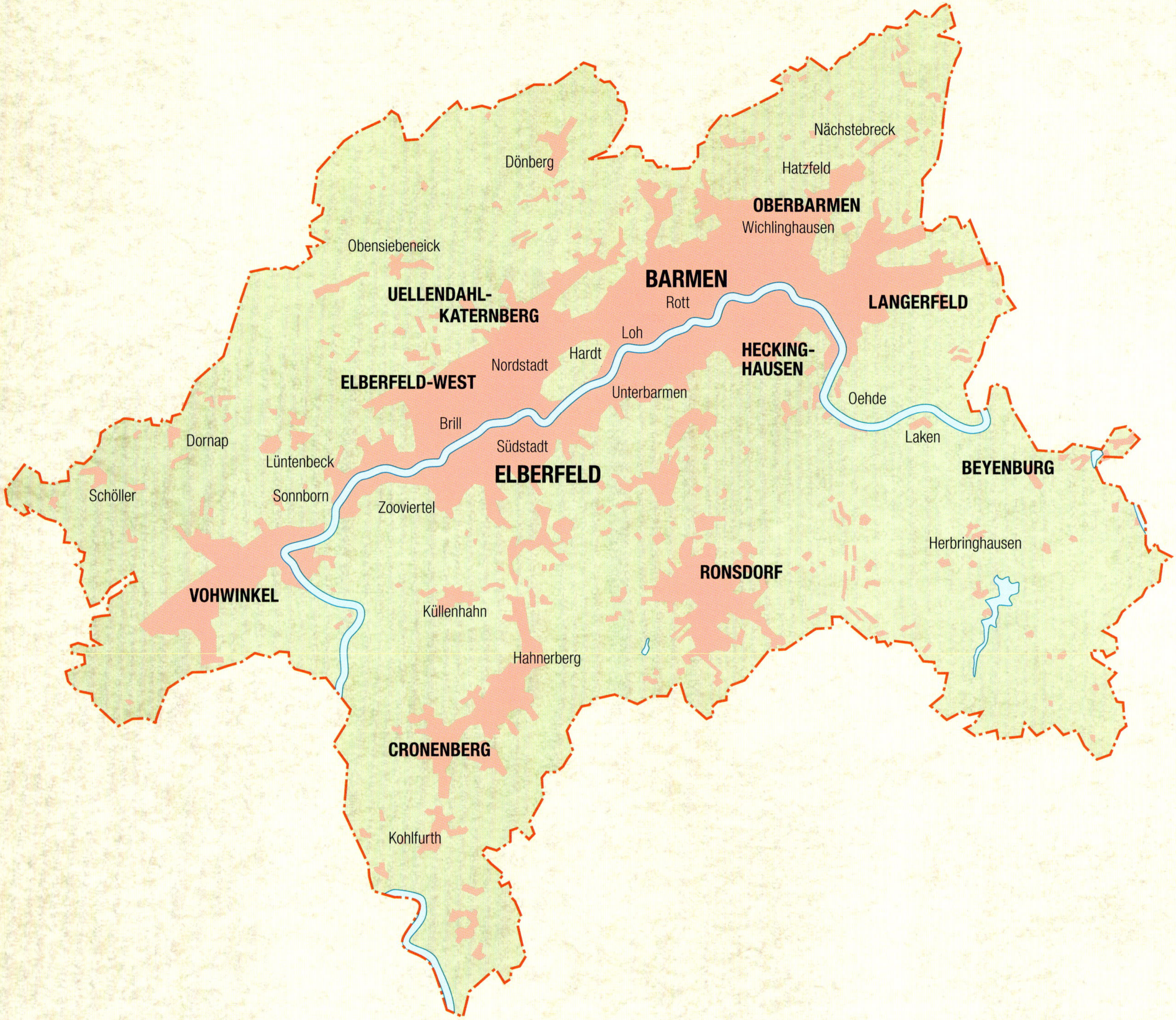

Nächstebreck
Dönberg
Hatzfeld
OBERBARMEN
Wichlinghausen
Obensiebeneick
BARMEN
UELLENDAHL-
KATERNBERG
Rott
LANGERFELD
Loh
HECKING-
HAUSEN
Hardt
Nordstadt
ELBERFELD-WEST
Unterbarmen
Oehde
Brill
Laken
Dornap
Südstadt
Lüntenbeck
BEYENBURG
ELBERFELD
Schöller
Sonnborn
Zooviertel
Herbringhausen
RONSDORF
VOHWINKEL
Küllenhahn
Hahnerberg
CRONENBERG
Kohlfurth